ZOO WITHOUT BARS

Zoo Without Bars is not only the story of
Chester Zoo, it is also the story of the
animals who live there. Animals like
Prince, the performing chimpanzee, who
came from a circus. Prince spent his first
few days turning cartwheels, while the rest
of the colony stared in amazement, then
tried to copy him, while he rocked with
laughter as they failed. He loved it when
crowds gathered, and would put on an
impressive one-chimp show. And Bobo, the
elephant, whose greed taught him cunning.
He took his place at the head of the
nightly queue for a loaf of bread, stuffed
it quickly into his mouth and doubled
back down the line to the back of the
queue, hopeful that the keeper might
overlook the first loaf and give him a
second.

3bcd

Zoo Without Bars

The story of Chester Zoo and its founder
George Saul Mottershead

June Johns

with photographs by
JACK SMITH

CAROUSEL EDITOR: ANNE WOOD

CAROUSEL BOOKS
A DIVISION OF TRANSWORLD PUBLISHERS LTD

ZOO WITHOUT BARS
A CAROUSEL BOOK 0 552 54051 X

Originally published in Great Britain
by Victor Gollancz Ltd.

PRINTING HISTORY

Victor Gollancz edition published 1969
Carousel edition published 1974

This book is set in Baskerville 12/13 pt.

Carousel Books are published by Transworld Publishers Ltd.,
Cavendish House, 57–59 Uxbridge Road, Ealing, London W.5

Made and printed in Great Britain by
Richard Clay (The Chaucer Press), Ltd., Bungay, Suffolk.

**NOTE: The Australian price appearing on the
back cover is the recommended retail price.**

TO JACK
for his unfailing encouragement,
help and enthusiasm

CONTENTS

LIST OF ILLUSTRATIONS

Between pages 80 *and* 81

CHAPTER ONE

AN OLD GREY ELEPHANT

The first elephant he ever saw made an indelible impression on George Saul Mottershead. He was eight years old in 1902 and the Boer War had just ended. To celebrate the victory his father, Albert Mottershead, a horticulturist from Sale in Cheshire, took George and his little brother Stanley for a day at the zoo.

Fascinated by the amusement park near by with its merry-go-rounds and side-shows, the children were reluctant to leave the gay booths for the gloomy animal houses. An elephant stood in a foul-smelling building, its face pressed up against thick iron bars between which it pushed its trunk to ring a bell. Onlookers were allowed to reward it with sweets and titbits.

The crowd laughed and children begged to be allowed to feed it, but George stood in silence, shocked and repelled, without understanding why. He had never seen a photograph of an elephant and had no idea what its natural habitat should be like, but his every instinct told him that this was all wrong.

Subdued, confused by his emotions, he allowed himself to be led round the rows of small cages of monkeys and chimps, but he alone was unamused by their antics.

His mother wanted to dose him with physic when he got home—he was not a moody boy and she felt sure he was sickening for something. But no medicine could remove the shame and indignation he felt on behalf of the elephant. He went into the garden where he kept his collection of finches, cockatiels and budgerigars in long aviaries, and looked at them with new eyes. He examined the tanks where his lizards and beetles lived, and the hen-cote of Plymouth Rock chickens. They had space to move freely, fresh air to breathe, and their cages smelled wholesomely clean.

His mind at rest, the little boy went back into the house for his suppper. Unable to formulate his reasons, but needing to confide his intentions, he blurted out: 'When I grow up I'm going to build a zoo ...' Bewildered by the outburst of laughter, he looked from his mother to his father, and added, under his breath, the most important of his plans. 'A zoo without bars.' But nobody heard, and his vow was not to be fulfilled until nearly thirty years later when the idea implanted by an old grey elephant resulted in Chester Zoo, one of the finest natural zoos in the world.

CHAPTER TWO

GROWING UP

Albert Mottershead, a well-known botanist and an authority on orchids, was delighted at the interest taken in his nursery gardens by his young son. He bought the child a few Plymouth Rock chickens and was so pleased at the care taken of them that he allowed George to keep the lizards and snakes that sometimes crawled out of imported parcels of rare orchids. Both mother and father were amused at the solemnity with which the boy cared for his collection. Instead of fondling them and, sometimes, forgetting them, he studied each creature daily and noticed how it responded to changes in the weather or diet.

But he would not have a dog. In the early 1900s the dogs of his acquaintance were usually to be found in yards and gardens at the end of chains. His abhorrence of the trappings of captivity was sufficient to drive him to extreme lengths, spending all his time and pocket money building bigger aviaries, more spacious tanks and larger runs for his pets. His younger brother, Stanley, was a great help when their father became seriously ill and George, aged thirteen, had to leave school to take full charge of the nursery business. He had worked with flowers for years and was quite able to take over completely for a few months, helped by his father when he had recovered sufficiently.

For three years George went to night school studying

accountancy and woodwork, both of which were to prove invaluable in later life. At sixteen he decided to leave the nursery and branch out into his own business: physical culture, a subject in which he had long been interested. He organised classes in the district and within two years was running three schools. Expansion was stopped by the First World War when he closed his schools and joined the South Lancashire Regiment, leaving his parents to look after his livestock.

In January 1916, George, then aged 21, married Elizabeth Atkinson, a Westmorland farmer's daughter. He went to France soon afterwards, but his army career came to an abrupt end when a bullet went through his neck, grazing the spinal chord and leaving him critically ill and completely paralysed.

He was still paralysed in December when they heard that Stanley, who had been in France for two years, had been killed in action. Frustrated at his inactivity, George could not bear to face the desolate future that now stretched interminably before him. He who had been so active was imprisoned in the cage of his immobile body. Where the elephant of his childhood rang a bell for food, he merely shouted. The simile was too exact to be amusing.

Haunted by dreams that refused to be abandoned, George was unable to remain indifferent to the much-reduced collection of birds and insects that had been tended lovingly by his father and his wife. Slowly he began to take an interest again. Marshalling all his strength and knowledge of physical training, he began teaching his muscles to obey his brain. It was hard and tedious, and frequently he almost gave up in despair. Then one day he found he could move his arms. Improvement was rapid and soon he was making his way round the nursery hobbling on crutches. A little later he surprised his doctors by discarding the crutches in favour of a stick. Within three years he could walk un-aided. True, he had a severe limp and became exhausted very quickly, but he felt whole again, ready to face the world.

On his doctor's advice, he and his wife and their baby daughter Muriel went to live in a farm cottage near Shavington, some miles from Crewe. On adjacent land he built a nursery and eventually bought a baby-linen shop in Crewe which he converted into a florist's, selling his produce direct to the public. It was an immediate success and as well as ploughing the profits back into the nursery, he indulged his hobby and bought some rare birds for his aviary.

When the milliner's shop next door became vacant, George bought it with the intention of expanding his own shop. But he had to buy the stock as well. As a large number of hats had already been ordered, he kept on two assistants to sell the stock. If he had not been so interested in his animals, he would have sold the nursery there and then and expanded the successful millinery business; but his sound commercial instinct was silenced by his love of living things. The hat shop closed, and became part of the florist's.

Meanwhile he had added a chimp and a few rare monkeys to his growing collection, and spent all his spare time studying their needs, enlarging their cages and giving them tree branches to simulate natural conditions. Each weekend he was inundated with sightseers who had heard of his nursery. Soon there were queues, and when he reluctantly turned visitors away because he had not the time to spare, people said they would willingly pay to see such an interesting collection so that a custodian could be employed to show them round.

While he was toying with the idea, one of the founders of the up-and-coming Crosville Motor Company came along with a proposition. If Mr Mottershead would open his zoo to the public, Crosville would run a special service to it each weekend. At that time Shavington had an infrequent bus service, and although it was not far from Crewe, few people had cars in those days.

The results were astounding. People came in their thousands from all parts of the North and Midlands, often repeating their visits as the collection grew. Bears were added, and more chimps, reptiles and exotic birds. Gradually George Mottershead began to realise that if ever he meant to make his dream zoo come true, he must have space. He had no idea what he would do for money; no idea how animals could be separated from the public except by bars. But he meant to find out. His search led him to Upton-by-Chester where 'Oakfield', a large, redbrick house, was for sale with nine acres of ornamental gardens and a fine courtyard of stables.

It was the beginning of an adventure that would send him twice round the world, that would make him a leading authority on animals in captivity, and that would free bears, elephants and chimps from the misery of being caged.

CHAPTER THREE

TROUBLE WITH BEARS

The week before the move was due to take place in December 1930, the Matlock Corporation wrote offering Mr Mottershead a pair of bears at a bargain price. They had bought them as cubs as an attraction for the town's 'Lover's Walk', a wooded area between the cliffs and the river. The bears had been housed in a large cave with a barred gate to its mouth, but having grown so big that they were too tall to stand erect, they had become more a liability than an attraction.

It was too good an offer to miss, especially as Mr Mottershead's existing collection of animals had been sold as fixtures of his nursery. The pair of Canadian black bears would therefore be the first exhibits in his new zoo.

He enlisted the aid of a friend, hired a truck and set off for Matlock with a couple of strong crates aboard. The crates had to be hauled over a footbridge to get them close to the bears' cave. Then the men began trying to entice the animals out with apples.

Eve lumbered out at once, grabbed her reward and was securely fastened into the crate. But Adam bared his fangs and retreated to the gloomy depths of the cave. While they coaxed and wheedled, Eve grew restless, beginning to resent her captivity. The crate groaned alarmingly and Mr Mottershead realised there was a danger of the timbers breaking under the strain.

'Let's leave the male for now,' he suggested, 'and take Eve back to Crewe where we can strengthen both crates.'

The motion of the truck seemed to soothe the captive bear and she stopped struggling. She was transferred to a spare cage at Crewe while both crates were reinforced with struts of wood and lined with sheet iron—protection against the long vicious claws.

Early next morning, both men set off again for Matlock, but Adam gave them no welcome. Having spent a cold, lonely night separated from his mate for the first time in his life, he was ready to do battle. Backwards and forwards he paced, his small eyes glinting wickedly, his forepaws ready to take a swipe at any intruder. All day the men tried, but by nightfall the bear was even more bad-tempered and determined to evade his captors.

Once again they returned home. The third morning was the last day they could spare. It was now or never. After a preliminary skirmish, they realised that bribes were getting them nowhere. They went to see the authorities. After all, they had brought up the bears —surely they would know the best way of handling them.

But no one had ever tried to catch the bears before. A vet was called in and his advice was greeted with relief. Tranquillizer drugs were put in the bear's food, and everyone stood well back to give him time to feed.

For hours he looked suspiciously at the dish, then, while the cluster of officials and George Mottershead and his companion held their breath, Adam began to eat. But instead of collapsing into unconsciousness, he seemed to have even more energy. To and fro he paced, his eyes never leaving the men.

'Let's try anaesthetic,' suggested the vet, eager to be off. The bear was obviously in fine condition and as he seemed to be impervious to the more gentle drugs, perhaps chloroform would subdue him for a few minutes.

But Adam sniffed it up as though it were perfume—and still he continued on the prowl.

One by one the crowd dispersed as darkness fell. The authorities ordered the floodlights to be switched on, bathing Lovers' Walk and the bears' den in light. Presently all had gone except Mr Mottershead and his friend. Refusing to accept defeat, they lugged the crate closer to the cave. There was only one thing for them to do; go into the den and get the bear out.

'Are you sure you want to?' Mr Mottershead asked his friend.

'Of course,' he replied. The bear snarled when the gate was opened, and tried to stand erect, the position bears adopt before attacking. But the roof was too low and he stumbled in an ungainly way on to all fours.

Each armed with an iron bar, the men first dragged the crate into the open doorway, then advanced on the bear. It was pitch black in the cave, and they trod gingerly, following the sound of the heavy grunts coming from the darkness. Not speaking, they edged shoulder to shoulder, round the cave, until they saw Adam silhouetted against the doorway. Again he tried to stand on his hindlegs and again he crashed his head against the roof. This time both men lunged at him and in an instant he had backed into the crate. They shot down the door, slid the bolt home and went out of the stinking den to the fresh air outside. It was after midnight and frost was glistening on the naked branches, but both men had to mop the perspiration from their foreheads.

Workmen had to be fetched to help drag the crate over the footbridge and heave it into the truck. They drove straight back to Chester to install Adam in his new home, a one-time horse box now lined with iron which stood in the courtyard behind the big house. He went in happily enough, exhausted by his three-day fight, and the two men went into the great empty house to sleep on camp beds for the night.

Early next morning George Mottershead went to get a paper to see what had been reported about his bears. He knew that several reporters had been following the capture, and he was delighted with the headline: 'Eve falls for the apple, but Adam won't bite.' It was just the sort of publicity he needed to get his new zoo started. On his way back up the lane he met an old man, one of the oldest residents of Upton, who had watched the comings and goings at Oakfield with interest.

'I'm sorry to hear of your trouble,' was his greeting. Thinking he was referring to the bear's stubbornness, Mr Mottershead explained that it was all over now, the bear was safely captured.

'Oh no, not that,' said the old man. 'I mean about the petition to stop you opening your zoo. A pity,' he shook his head sadly. 'I'd have liked it, myself.' And he ambled off, leaving Mr Mottershead shaken to the core. He had sunk all his capital into Oakfield and dared not contemplate such a setback. He shook away his unease and decided that the old man had made a mistake. But just to be on the safe side, he hastened into Chester two miles away to see his bank manager who would soon dispel the rumour.

But it was true. Residents of the select neighbourhood of Upton had no wish to be invaded by dirty wild animals. They had raised a petition which was signed by many worthy citizens of the city, demanding that permission to run a zoo be withheld.

'I can assure you that my animals won't be dirty,' Mr Mottershead protested.

But no one wanted to hear. They stuck to their refusal and the zoo—unopened—had to bide its time until a public enquiry was held in Chester Town Hall in

February 1931.

Mr Mottershead heard the protests and he answered every one. He did not intend to build an ugly ten-foot brick wall round his property. He did not intend to install dirt-track racing or hurdy-gurdies. He planned to have gardens where animals could live in natural surroundings, without bars wherever possible. It sounded like madness back in 1931, and many residents predicted slaughter when wild animals invaded the district.

But after five or six weeks the Ministry of Health announced their verdict in favour of the new zoo.

Mr and Mrs Mottershead, their daughters, Muriel, now fourteen, and June aged four, and Grandfather Mottershead, began working to get ready for the grand opening at Easter. The exhibits were pitifully few. Adam and Eve, the bears, half a dozen assorted monkeys, some the gifts of people who had kept them as pets but had tired of them and a small collection of birds.

Nevertheless they wrought wonderful changes in those first four months. Grandfather took charge of the gardens and the conservatory where he planned to grow tropical plants. Mrs Mottershead opened a café and refreshment room on the ground floor of the big house, and Muriel became the zoo's first keeper. She cleaned out every cage daily, fed and watered the animals under her father's supervision, and waited for the crowds of people who were needed to put the zoo on its feet.

The opening was a complete flop. Groups of three or four people came. Then there were no more for hours. Sometimes two or three days went by before a solitary visitor came.

'Stop worrying,' Mr Mottershead told his family when their spirits were at rock bottom. 'It'll take time.' And his immovable confidence invariably gave them

21

new heart.

The people who came were mostly from places outside Chester. The townsfolk had not forgiven Mr Mottershead for the rejection of their petition and they were a long time in facing facts and realising that the zoo had come to stay. Those who had seen other zoos were intrigued by this one. They asked questions. 'Are birds happier having long cages in which they can fly, instead of cosy little cages where they just hop from perch to perch?'

Mr Mottershead explained his theories, and visitors came again and again to follow the progress of the struggling zoo.

In 1932 Chester Zoo bought the collection of animals and birds that had been taken over by the successor at Shavington. The owner had not had the former success and now wanted to sell the collection. Mr Mottershead went to inspect the animals, among which was a new specimen: the dirtiest, most bedraggled polar bear imaginable.

Punch glowered through the bars of his decrepit, corrugated iron shed. Crouching on the tiny patch of concrete that was his floor, he hadn't enough spirit to make a bid for freedom. Mr Mottershead stared back at him, taking in the ridiculously tiny water dish, hardly deep enough for the bear to have a good drink. He could not really afford to keep a polar bear. Already his wife was having to buy animal food out of her housekeeping money, but he hadn't the heart to say 'no'. He had visions of bankruptcy and ruin, but he could not condemn the bear to one more week of such misery.

To begin with, Punch was housed in the old laundry building while Mr Mottershead built a den with an open-air run and a small bath. The bath was absurdly small, he knew, but with so little money to spare for cement and sand and metal, it was the best he could do.

And it was just big enough for the bear to bathe in.

Punch slunk into his new quarters and flopped at the back of his den, taking no notice of his new run and his bath.

'Come on,' the girls begged. 'Have a bath and maybe you'll look like a real polar bear.' But Punch had forgotten the habits he must have learned long ago in the clean snows and icy seas of the Arctic. He had spent most of his life in a circus where water had no place, and he had no intention of changing his habits now. His diet had, of necessity, to be restricted to the cheapest meat from the knackers' yard, and month by month, Punch gulped down his rations, retreated to his corner, and grew dirtier and dirtier until visitors were sure he was a black bear trading under false colours.

A day that was to be of importance to Punch began as an ordinary autumn Saturday when the local hunt held its point-to-point race in Upton. It started just outside the zoo's main gate and at the first jump a magnificent horse fell and broke its neck. It had to be shot immediately, and one of the officials called at the zoo to see if they could make use of the carcass. Could they!

Mr Mottershead found the sharpest knives and axe in the house, and went across to the field to see what he could do. Piece by piece he butchered the horse into movable portions which he then hauled to Oakfield's cool, slate-slabbed wine cellars.

Then he took a choice hunk of rump and tossed it to Punch. For a second the bear stared unbelievingly before falling on the meat and tearing it to bits. After his usual way of gulping down food as though it had no taste, it was a delight to watch his enjoyment. The next day he had a similar meal, and the next and the next, until all the meat had gone a month or so later.

It was the turning point in Punch's life, and, ultimately in the future of the zoo. He began to sit up and take notice. He rolled over in the open air, waving his gigantic paws like a puppy. He stretched to his full height and stamped from side to side, perhaps remembering the tricks he had once performed to the sound of applause. He became strong and healthy. But he absolutely refused to have anything to do with water.

CHAPTER FOUR

A LION AT LARGE

When the zoo had been open for two years, the accounts made sorry reading. They had not had as many visitors as had used to visit Shavington in one month. Life was one long struggle: coping with the care of the animals, the maintenance of the property and the cultivation of the grounds. The Mottershead family had not had a day off since they had arrived, and even six-year-old June was expected to help.

A realist, Mr Mottershead knew that his dream needed a miracle to get it off the ground. He sat down and tried to work out ways and means of achieving success without compromising his ideals. In his zoo, he maintained, animals must come first. The easy way would have been to commercialise it, add an amusement park, or even make the animals earn their keep by performing, by having chimps' tea parties or dressing the monkeys in clothes.

At no time did he even consider it. The animals in his zoo must be allowed to retain their innate dignity. Ahead of his time, he longed for the day when the public would realise that zoos were not places where people could laugh at animals, and perhaps elevate and comfort their own egos in the process.

Yet it was obvious that it could not make a profit. The answer he came up with was that of making it a non-profit-making zoo run by a society. Delighted, and full of hope, he began writing letters to local dignitaries, leading citizens and industrialists, explaining his scheme and aims, and inviting them to join. It was hoped that such people would support the society, perhaps by lending it money until such time as it was self-supporting, when all the profits could be ploughed back.

Locally the response was negligible, but a few interested people came from Manchester and Liverpool. Of these, several offered to lend money, but only at a high rate of interest which the zoo could not have afforded. After many difficulties and setbacks, the North of England Zoological Society was registered under the Companies Act as a non-profit-sharing company to be operated as a charitable, educational institution on May 9th 1934. On June 13th 1934 the Society took over the runnning of the zoo. Members were invited, the annual subscription being one guinea a year, which entitled the holder to free admission at any time. But they were slow in joining. As the debts mounted, the Society issued debentures in multiples of twenty-five pounds and although the first balance sheet showed receipts totalling £1,120, there was a deficit of £213.

Nevertheless George Mottershead continued to study the needs of his animals and to expand the zoo. At that time the Duke of Westminster lived on his estate near Chester, Eaton Hall, and was a keen naturalist. He presented the zoo with a capybara, the largest rodent in existence and a native of Brazil. Miss Esther Holt, of the shipping family, gave a magnificent collection of rare birds, and one of the founder members of the Society, Miss Geraldine Russell Allen, paid for an aquarium to be built in the basement of the house.

In one of the three sections of the conservatory, where Grandfather Mottershead reared tropical plants, flowers and ferns, a long flight cage was built, another section was equipped for snakes and filled with plants over which they could crawl as if in their natural habitat; and two baby alligators were installed in the centre pond.

Outside, areas of paddock were turned over to pelicans, flamingoes and cranes that soon learnt to ignore the low wire fences and take themselves off for a walk whenever it suited them. There were so few visitors that the animals virtually had the zoo to themselves, and they lost no time in establishing ownership. One pelican used to anticipate meals, waddle up to the back door of the house, and squawk until his fish was produced. The same bird liked to stretch his wings in flight and one day an employee of the Duke of Westminster telephoned to say that an extra pelican had appeared among the Duke's pelicans on the serpentine at Eaton Hall: would Mr Mottershead be good enough to drive over and collect it? But by the time he had crossed Chester and arrived at Eaton Hall, the pelican was winging its way home and had reached the zoo before he got back.

As the birds settled down and began to breed, the value of the stock increased proportionately and the newcomers were exchanged for new specimens of birds and animals from other zoos. Two lion cubs were among the additions and although they were raised to maturity, they died in their second year. Bristol Zoo, hearing of their death and wishing to help the small emergent zoo, presented it with three young lionesses, Faith, Hope and Charity. Soon a male, Patrick, came from Ireland to found a magnificent pride of lions that were to be exported all over the world, even to Africa, in the coming years.

Patrick lost favour with June very soon after his arrival. She had a small black terrier, Jet, that had been brought up in the zoo without fear of wild animals. One day he unearthed a rat and chased it round the courtyard. The rat fled into Patrick's cage, and Jet followed, squeezing himself beneath the lower bar. The rat got away but Jet was killed with one swipe of the lion's paw. June was inconsolable. She swore she hated all lions and would have nothing more to do with them.

A friend of her father bought her a Sealyham, Peter, and advised her to make sure he developed a healthy respect for larger animals. Determined that no accident should befall him, June introduced Peter to the youngest lion cubs, taking him with her whenever she went into the cubs' den to play with them. Peter enjoyed these rough and tumbles and would often prefer to fall asleep with his favourite cub, Mowgli, instead of going into the house with his young mistress.

By the time Mowgli was fully grown and June could no longer go into his cage, Peter had formed a friendship for life. The small dog and the huge lion shared the same quarters, water dish and food. Peter would go on an expedition round the neighbourhood and return towards evening, dirty, tired and hungry, to Mowgli's cage. The lion would lick him clean until the shaggy white fur was spotless, then he would let the dog nestle up to him and sleep undisturbed all night.

It was a beautiful friendship—one in which June had no part. Peter no longer wanted to come into the house, and Mowgli would have nothing to do with the other lions.

Mr Mottershead decided to wean them from each other so that they could live more normal lives. But when he took Peter away, the lion sulked and refused to eat. After two or three attempts to keep the dog away by persuasion, it became necessary to confine him in a pen of his own some distance from Mowgli so that they could not call to each other. For a few days it appeared that the separation had been successful, then Mowgli began to wilt and within a few days had pined to death.

Now, more than ever, Peter had to be kept penned

up so that he could not explore the other lions' cages in search of Mowgli. But the dog had other ideas. One night he tunnelled his way out, but instead of surfacing on the path outside his pen, he came up in the compound next to him where a pack of dingoes lived. He was killed instantly, and this time June vowed she would never have another dog.

That winter pneumonia attacked the chimps, and Muriel, helped by her mother, took charge of the invalids. For weeks they did not have a full night's sleep, for as fast as one chimp recovered, another became ill.

Sickness seldom comes singly, and one of the lionesses due to cub in a few weeks came into labour. The first cub was stillborn, and just as the second was born, the mother died.

'We'll never rear it,' said Mott sadly. He held the tiny wet mewling bundle, its eyes firmly closed, and wondered what he should do.

'Let me have it, Daddy,' begged June. 'I'll feed it. I've always helped Muriel with the baby animals, so I know what to do.'

It was either that or putting it down immediately, and he decided to give his daughter the chance. A warm bed was made in a box in one of the many spare rooms in the big house, and June took full charge. Although the house was equipped with central heating, they could not afford to run it, so all the rooms were equally cold. But June cared for the cub as no animal had ever been cared for before. To begin with she fed it with a baby's bottle every two hours, decreasing to three, then four hours as the animal grew stronger. At first June nursed it like a baby, with a bib round its neck and a napkin round its bottom.

To everyone's surprise, Christy, as June called her, not only survived, but positively thrived on the treatment. At three months she came when called and was fully house trained. She was devoted to June and used to cry when she went off to school each morning, padding round the house all day until she came home each evening. At six months she was too big to stay in the house and had to go in a cage.

'She had better go in with the other lions so that she can have someone to play with,' said Mr Mottershead. But Christy had other ideas. She pinned her ears against her head and swore like a giant cat when she saw where she was about to be put.

'All right then, we'll put you in a cage of your own,' decided Mr Mottershead.

But still Christy was not happy. She wanted to be in the house, and every time she was put into her cage she would whine and cry until June went in and put her arms round the lion's neck. Unfortunately June could not live in the cage with her, and visitors began approaching the two full-time keepers to ask what was wrong with the miserable howling lioness.

Every evening when the visitors had gone, June would open the cage door and let Christy bound out, bowling her over with an affectionate pat. Like a dog, she followed at heel, occasionally knocking June off her feet when she rubbed against her legs. Sometimes she would jump up, putting her dinner-plate sized paws on June's shoulders and sending her flying, but not once did she unsheath her claws or try to bite her.

As Christy grew older, Mott realised that there was trouble ahead. He could understand the lioness's indignation at being put in a cage after a life of freedom. At the same times, lions are not kittens to be kept in the house. He gave instructions that Christy must not be let out unless he was there to see that no accident occurred. At the back of his mind was the ever-present fear of an animal running amok in the village and harming not only the local population, but also the fragile status of the zoo.

June sought an ally in her mother, and together, when Father was out, they would take Christy for a walk round the zoo and play with her for an hour in the evening. When Father was due back they would take her to her cage. But the lioness would not always co-operate. She would dig in her heels and refuse to move, and they would have to grab a forepaw each and, backing into the cage themselves, would haul in the reluctant lioness.

One evening when June was out, Mrs Mottershead took Christy with her on her evening round while she fed titbits to the animals and saw that they were all right for the night. She found she had run out of bread, and a little fallow deer was expecting some. She left it playing with Christy while she went back to the house for some more. On her return the deer was still there, but no Christy.

'Come on, Christy, where are you?' she called. But there was no answering grunt. She looked behind the clumps of azaleas where June and the lioness used to play hide-and-seek, but still no Christy. Alarmed, she returned to the house to alert her husband and the resident keeper who lived with his wife in the upstairs rooms.

They scattered over the nine acres calling and listening for an answering growl. By this time the other animals had realised something was wrong and were prowling and chattering and calling to the keepers. The search was extended to adjacent land where a field of corn stood waist high. But there was not a ripple to show the path of the lioness.

Meanwhile Muriel, who had been out, returned to the house and found nobody in. She went upstairs and there, coming out of a bedroom, was Christy, unaware of the panic ouside. She had wandered in after Mrs

Mottershead, strolled upstairs and entered the room occupied by the resident keeper, where she found a baby girl asleep in a cot. While everyone was in the grounds, Christy had made a thorough inspection of the cot and its occupant but had neither harmed nor even woken the baby.

She had proved her reliability, but she had also proved the folly of allowing a fully grown lioness to wander about at will. This time there had been no harm done—but next time? Mr Mottershead explained to his daughter that he could not risk having Christy shot, as she would be if she were to roam outside the zoo. He proposed to put her in the main lion enclosure where she might realise that she was, after all, a lioness, and settle down to raise a family and take her mind off humans.

Christy had to be hauled to the enclosure the next day, and immediately she set on the first lion that approached her. The other lions joined in the free-for-all and Mott had visions of all his valuable animals wiping each other out. In a thunder of growls and roars, Christy escaped from the scrum and fled up a tree, challenging the others to dare follow.

Mott saw his chance. He told the keepers to put meat in the dens to entice the lions in so that they could be shut off from the paddock. But the lions weren't co-operating. They ignored the extra rations and paraded round the foot of the tree, baring their teeth at the intruder aloft. Determined to prevent slaughter, Mott picked up a pitchfork and went into the enclosure. The lions ceased their pacing and stood snarling at him.

Ignoring Christy, and hoping that she had not reverted to nature, he walked slowly forward, bunching the lions together and heading them for their dens. One tried to make a break, but Mott was there with his pitchfork. He hoped he would not have to use it—and as it happened, he didn't; but if need be he would have jabbed the lion rather than give up and let them fight it out among themselves.

His courage worked. The lions were locked up and Christy came down from her perch, still whisking her tail like a metronome gone mad. She went back to her cage and her heart-rending yowling, but her days in Chester were numbered. Mott realised that he could do no good with her and that she would most probably fret herself to death if she were not allowed to see June every day. The only solution was to remove her to another zoo where she could start life again and, if possible, forget her mistress.

It was a heartbreaking decision for the whole family, but particularly for June. She wept and pleaded and it was a long time before she could bring herself to accept the inevitability of the parting.

'I shall never let myself get fond of an animal again,' she sobbed. And, indeed, Christy was a never-to-be-forgotten lesson for Mott himself. To humanise an animal to such an extent that it could not identify itself with its own breed was a mistake he would not make again. Christy went to a continental dealer, but the love she left behind her was to save thousands of animals from a similar anguish in the future.

CHAPTER FIVE

TAKE DOWN THE BARS

One day a pair of Mandrills, baboons from West Africa, arrived as a gift from the Holt family. About two feet high and half grown, the hideous pair were just developing the violently red faces and behinds that distinguish them from the rest of the baboon family. Mott installed them in a large cage where they settled down immediately. Like most of the residents, they enjoyed excellent health, sailed through the winter without so much as a sneeze, and the male's face grew redder and redder as he reached maturity. There was never occasion to bring the vet in to see them, and they accepted whatever fruit was fed to them, depending on the financial situation prevailing from month to month.

One morning when he made his first rounds of the day, looking at every animal in turn, Mott was surprised when the Mandrills set up an excited chitter-chatter as he approached. Usually they might turn a few somersaults, or even fling fruit peel at him by way of greeting, but they had never before sounded such an alarm. He hurried to their cage. They were sitting huddled together in one corner, leaning against the wall, and on the female's knee was a baby. Mott looked closer, unable to believe his eyes. Mandrills had never before been known to breed in captivity, yet here was a perfectly formed newly born baby, its near-human hands clinging to its mother, its shoe-button eyes staring at him in alarm.

Jubilant, he went to tell the family and the keepers, and to warn them to keep well away from the cage so as not to disturb the new arrival. In addition, extra food was to be given so that the mother would not become undernourished. Daily Mott trod carefully, hoping that the baby would neither be abandoned by its mother nor attacked by its father, both fairly common occurrences among baboons. But the infant thrived, and as it grew stronger the parents forgot their fears and welcomed human contact again.

Encouraged in his belief that animals were healthier and happier in conditions as near natural as possible, Mott began considering ways and means of making a new lion enclosure without bars. He toyed with the idea of surrounding the paddock with a deep ditch across which they would not be able to leap to freedom. The area he had selected was not quite an acre, but the ditch would have to measure at least thirty feet across for safety. It left very little room in which the lions could exercise.

At that time the Society was administered by an elected council of twenty-one members who met regularly to discuss ways of keeping the zoo on its feet and to make plans for its development. After hearing Mott's views, they tentatively agreed that if the lions could be held captive by a ditch, then they had no objection.

One of the members, Lord Leverhulme, was keen to help, and he laid the foundation stone in 1937. But meanwhile Mott had been going over his plans. He was rearing a fine pride of lions and he could not bear to think of their future being threatened by too small an enclosure. He discussed the problem with his friend, Cedric Flood, then Director of Dublin Zoo, who shared his opinion that animals required far more freedom than they had been getting in zoos all over the world.

'Mott,' he said, 'if only you, or someone else, would have the courage to put lions behind high, chain-linked fencing, it would revolutionise the lives of captive animals for all time. I'm sure they wouldn't escape. But it would take courage to put it to the test.'

With nine acres of land altogether, and only one that could be allocated to the lions, a thirty-foot wide ditch seemed a colossal waste of space. Mott drew up new plans and put them before his council, explaining that instead of condemning the animals to a tiny plateau, he meant to give them all the ground; space enough to roam and play, space enough that the grass would not be worn bare, and that instead of a ditch, a twelve-foot high fence with a two-foot inward overhang of chain-link would keep them in.

The meeting was in uproar.

'What's wrong with bars?' demanded one irate member. 'All the other zoos in the world can't be wrong, and they all use bars. Why must you be different?'

'Chain-link fencing!' they scoffed. 'It's lions you're keeping, man. Not chickens!'

But Mott would not budge. He let the storm rage over his head, listening to the complaints that he had been hearing all his life. He laughed to himself when he heard first one, then another, warn him that lions were not to be trusted. As if anyone knew better than he! Just a few days before a young keeper had come gasping to the house.

'The lions' door,' he panted, 'it's off its pulley.'

Mott had hastened to the dens and had found that the door was jammed, partially open. It had been wrongly handled and had slipped off its top runner. It could only be fixed from inside the cage and Mott knew that only he dared do it. The young keeper was so nervous that the lions would have made mincemeat of him had he stepped inside with them.

Carrying a stepladder and not turning his back for one instant on the five prowling and growling lions, Mott edged into the cage, set up the ladder and slowly climbed up it backwards. Any sudden move might have startled them into springing at him, and he had no illusions about the outcome; there was no one to whom he could call for help. The lions were snarling at the intrusion and Mott had to keep his eyes on them, while above his head his hands felt for the jammed mechanism and manoeuvred it back into position. The whole operation took perhaps five minutes, each second of which seemed a lifetime. But it was the sort of experience that made him lost patience with those whose only bleat was that one must not take chances.

Again and again Mott explained to the Council that lions were not squirrels, that they could not climb twelve-foot fences and that, even if they developed prehensile tails and so were able to perform such a feat, they would not want to leave. Everyone howled with laughter, even those members of the Council who were willing to try the scheme. But Mott would not give an inch; his whole life's work was in danger of being destroyed if he compromised. This, he told himself, was only the beginning of his fight to free animals from bars. If his Council would not let lions live behind wire, how could they ever be expected to let chimps live on islands, elephants walk without chains and all the other dreams which he was keeping secret until he could find ways of making them come true.

The Council could not agree, and almost half of them threatened to resign unless Mott abandoned his plans. But Mott surprised them by accepting their resignations. The only hitch was that the war was to come before he had time to build his wife-fenced lion run.

When it became certain that war was not far off,

many members felt that the zoo could not survive yet more difficulties. Although the membership of the Society had increased, so had the annual deficit, and although there were many more exhibits, each one meant an extra mouth to feed, an extra cage to clean out.

Determined not to give up, Mott put forward an adoption scheme under which members of the public could 'adopt' an animal, pay for its keep, and in return have their name on a card by the animal's cage. It sounded gimmicky. Why should the public be interested in having their names attached to monkeys, birds and bears? But it was not rejected out of hand. Instead it lay in abeyance, to be used only in case of desperate necessity as a last resort.

In September 1939 war was declared and the adoption scheme was made public. For some while Mott had made regular broadcasts on the BBC Children's Hour, talking about Chester Zoo. He had a wide following and his animals and their individual characters were well known to his radio audience, many of whom had not been able to visit the zoo. Now he could estimate just how great was the public interest in animals. Within weeks people from all over Britain had put down their names specifying what kind of animal they wished to 'adopt'. Small creatures, including some monkeys, cost a shilling a week; chimps were five shillings, lions ten shillings and bears a pound. The small amounts rolled in with clockwork regularity and Mott breathed more easily as he paid his bills.

An elderly lady from the Lake District telephoned to ask if she might visit the zoo on her way back from a holiday in North Wales. It was, as usual, a quiet day at the zoo when she arrived and Mott took her round, telling her about each animal. When she came to the polar bear, she halted and looked more closely.

'What a disgustingly dirty animal!' Miss Catherine Jane Tompkyns-Grafton was a keen and well-informed naturalist and she had always believed that polar bears liked water.

'He needs a pool,' she went on. 'Why hasn't he been provided with one?'

Mott explained his financial position, adding that he had done his best by giving Punch the little pool, but that he had refused to use it. She accepted that nothing could be done to build a large pool, especially as war-time restrictions had already come into force, but she offered to 'adopt' Punch and pay a pound a week for his keep for the rest of the war.

As well as finding a sponsor, Punch gained a playmate when Butlin's Holiday Camp at Skegness was taken over for military purposes and the private zoo had to be evacuated. Would Chester take the collection which included, among other things, five leopards and a female polar bear? More stables were converted and when the convoy of animals arrived, everyone held their breath when Punch was introduced to Judy. She was just as white as he was black.

They sniffed at each other, rubbed shoulders, then Judy manoeuvred herself into the tiny bathtub to wash off the dust of the journey. The bystanders hoped that Punch would catch on and clean himself, but it was not to be. He watched with interest each time Judy had a bath but he could not be persuaded to try it himself.

Always fierce, Punch became more so now that he had a companion, and keepers were warned to take no chances. Cleaning out the den presented difficulties as it had been built for one bear and there was only one trap cage into which Punch had been coaxed—and locked —while the enclosure was cleaned out each day. Now Judy went into the trap, leaving Punch at large in the area which had to be cleaned. Mott took over the job himself, and had the keeper standing by the outer gate, ready to close it the instant Mott had finished and climbed through.

All went well, Punch being content to stand by the trap cage looking at Judy through the railings while Mott hosed and swept the run. But one day the keeper absent-mindedly shut the outer door while Mott was still inside. Punch grabbed the chance to launch an attack. The stone wall was fourteen feet high and Mott was nearly fifty years of age, but he scaled the sides as if he were a Commando. He managed to grasp the top ledge while his feet sought a hold in the sheer wall. Punch leapt and grabbed his shoe, and in the ensuing struggle the entire sole came off, causing Punch to fall backwards. In the split second's delay, Mott managed to scramble to safety.

Now that troops were garrisoned in and around Chester, a new breed of visitor became frequent. Bored, lonely and hard-up, the men came often and many were deeply interested in the progress of the animals, even to the extent of seeking out Mott to ask him searching questions about their habits. Very few acts of wanton cruelty were committed at the zoo, but one that stands out— and to this day remains unsolved—is the murder of the pelicans.

As well as their own three, the zoo was presented with four pelicans belonging to the Duke of Westminster who felt they could be better looked after in the zoo during the war. One morning on his rounds, Mott found a pelican lying dead by the fence. He went into the enclosure and found, in various places, all seven birds dead. An examination showed that each had been given a powder-impregnated cottonwool puff of a type sold for cosmetic purposes by large stores. Ever trusting, the pelicans had taken them from a visitor, and each had choked as the puff stuck in its throat. An empty box which had contained the powder puffs was found near-by. It had been a deliberately planned act of murder.

Feeding at the zoo became a problem when supplies of essentials virtually dried up overnight. Tropical birds that had been fed exclusively on exotic fruit and grain at first turned up their beaks when offered English soft fruits—and damaged stuff at that. Local stores in Chester rallied round to save their squashed fruit, scraps and broken biscuits which Mott collected each day. There was some danger that the creatures might be unable to adapt their needs and die of starvation. In particular, the Malayan sun bears that had lived on Nestle's condensed milk were now offered broken biscuits and fruit. After a brief display of temper, they accepted the change philosophically and began to thrive on their new diet. Horse meat, the staple food of the carnivores, rose in price, but at least it was always available.

Zoos in the front line in the event of invasion, such as Bristol and Paignton, evacuated some of their animals to Chester and although both June and Muriel Mottershead helped out, there was a serious shortage of labour. When it became obvious that every able-bodied man and woman in the country would soon be directed to work, some young people, whose education had not prepared them to earn their own living, began looking for congenial work. They came to Chester Zoo.

Looking back, Mott believes that some of the girls who had never so much as washed a teacup were among the best workers he had ever seen, before or since. One such girl, who had been in a Paris finishing school at the outbreak of war, arrived to start work in the family chauffeur-driven Rolls-Royce. She shared a bedroom in the old house with several other girls from mixed backgrounds; she mucked out the chimps' cages as they had never been cleaned before, and never once complained of the frequently arduous and extremely tiring work. Others were not so capable. One girl almost killed off an entire tank of tropical fish when she filled it up with icy cold water. All three Mottershead women had to come to the rescue, heating water on the kitchen stove and rushing with it down to the cellar to raise the temperature in the tank before the fish froze to death.

Air raids became quite a problem, for although very few bombs fell near Chester, it was no distance from Liverpool and Manchester, both of which experienced many savage bombing attacks. For the safety of everyone living near the zoo, it was a rule that whenever enemy aircraft were approaching, all the animals had to be locked into their interior pens, as the fences of their open-air enclosures might be knocked down if the zoo had a direct hit. In addition, Mott had to carry a loaded gun and patrol the grounds whenever the air raid siren sounded an alert. This happened so frequently that at times he was managing to get only two or three hours' sleep a night and still having to do a full day's work, seven days a week, fifty-two weeks a year.

Early in 1941 Mott received a telephone call from a theatrical agent. At the outbreak of war, two elephants and their mahout attached to Dourley's Tropical Express Revue, a German-Argentinian concern, had been isolated in Britain, separated from the main body of the show on the Continent. The keeper had been wandering about Britain with his two elephants, unable to find them permanent accommodation and regular food, and not knowing where to turn. He spoke very little English and was now stranded in Northampton. The elephants had been upset by air raids and Kay, the mahout, was so concerned about their safety that he had started to sleep with them so that he could soothe them when the bombs began to fall.

Mott and his workers rushed round improvising an elephant house by using the stone arch leading into the courtyard as a roof span and building on to it.

Molly and Mannikin, both Singalese, moved into their new home. At some time during their travels round Europe they had been badly frost-bitten about the ears, and bits had rubbed off, making them even smaller than usual. Extra food was bought to try to get them back into condition, but Mannikin was too weak and died soon after her arrival. But Molly, whose reputation for humorous savagery followed her round on her travels, soon recovered her strength and her temper. Kay, too, was run down with his hardship and he went down with a severe attack of 'flu that kept him in bed. He fought to get up, pleading to be with his elephant, but Mott was adamant: doctor's orders were meant to be followed to the letter. He took over the feeding and watering of Molly.

He had heard many accounts of the number of people Molly had severely injured—and perhaps killed—back in Ceylon when they were careless enough to enter her stall and put themselves in a position where Molly could crush them against a wall. Mott had so far never gone into the stall without Kay, and he carried the first bucket of water carefully, keeping the open door directly behind him. Molly dipped her trunk into the bucket, drew up all the water and, instead of pouring it into her mouth, sprayed it right into Mott's face, with the force of a fireman's hosepipe. He tried again, with the same result. And she absolutely refused to eat anything, no matter what sort of delicacy it was. If Kay would not feed her, then she would prefer to starve. In two days he was out of bed, and Molly dropped her hunger strike. She had been trained in Ceylon by Kay when he was a child of ten. They had grown up together and her dependence on him was absolute. Each day, if no visitors were about, he would take her out of her stall, unshackle her leg chain and take her into the now neglected orchard.

Mott watched fascinated as the huge elephant frolicked and pranced, occasionally knocking down an apple or plum tree by accident. Kay would make her stay in one spot while he went to the far end of the orchard. Then he would call her, and she obeyed at once, lumbering up to him and giving him a playful cuff with her trunk.

She had been trained to give rides to children who were strapped into a double-sided chair on her back, and during the summer months she spent most of the day strolling round the zoo accompanied by Kay and a swarm of children. She picked her way carefully among them and never showed irritation. But a drunken man who put in an appearance and began staggering in front of her pointing his finger at her and jeering about 'pink elephants' was too much. First she shoved him aside with her trunk, and when he returned to annoy her, she hoiked him up by the back of his pants and held him suspended at trunk-length, dangling five feet above the ground. The crowds who had collected to watch gasped, afraid that she would crash him to the ground and trample on him. During the few moments while Molly was deciding what to do with him, the man became sobered by fear. Then, slowly and very gently, she walked to the grass verge and deposited him on the ground. Everyone cheered, and while he scuttled away, Molly was showered with titbits and praise.

Some time later when Kay married and had a daughter, the child became the apple of Molly's eye; she regarded the little girl as her own. The child's favourite game was to toddle into the elephant stall and sit on Molly's trunk which the elephant curved to form a swing. They would play together for hours and the animal's devotion was touching.

The child rode a tricycle round the zoo and one day, when Molly was giving rides, the little girl ran her tricycle into a paddock fence and got the wheel jammed. She let out a howl as she struggled to free herself, and from the other side of the zoo, Molly heard the cry. She broke away from Kay, and while the load of children aboard clung to their seat, Molly lumbered across the lawns, threading her way between the trees, the branches of which whipped overhead, going as fast as she could to the distressed child. For once she ignored Kay's frantic commands and did not stop until she reached the child and assured herself that she was all right. Then she nuzzled the little girl with her trunk, soothing and consoling until Kay caught up with them and released the offending tricycle.

She was not so considerate to Mott. Like most zoos, Chester was troubled with mice; but unlike most zoos, did not encourage cats. Years before Mott had connected the high incidence of infection with the large number of cats as they are great carriers of disease. Even when they did not go into cages, they rubbed against fences and succeeded in spreading illness from animal to animal. Once he had banned cats from the zoo, there was a dramatic decrease in both disease and deaths. Accordingly, he had to fight rats and mice with traps.

Molly's enclosure was bordered by a ditch over which she could not stride, and in the bottom of the ditch, out of reach of her ever-enquiring trunk, were mouse traps. One day, Mott was crawling on all fours along the ditch collecting the traps when Molly bent down and grabbed him by his clothes in the small of his back. For perilous seconds she held him aloft and he was unable to move. He dared not shout in case she dropped him on to the concrete below. On the other hand he knew she was quite capable of either tossing him over her head or setting him down to trample him. She did none of these. She put him right on the edge of the ditch and stood there laughing to herself as he hastily rolled down the side and crawled away before she could change her mind and think up more tricks.

Molly had a wicked sense of humour which she practised on everyone except Kay and his daughter, and if anything had happened to either of them, there would have been no controlling her.

Once again Mott vowed that he would never train animals to depend on one human being. It was too great a responsibility for the man, and a great unkindness to the animal who would not be able to understand if a parting became necessary.

Fortunately Molly was able to be near her beloved mahout until the hour of her death. She developed arthritis and although every known treatment, including that by sun-ray lamp, was tried, she was in such pain that the vet had to put her down in 1955, after fourteen years in Chester Zoo.

CHAPTER SIX

PUNCH TAKES A BATH

Two of the oldest residents of the zoo were a pair of Griffon vultures which Mott had bought back from his successor at Shavington. Right from the beginning he had installed them in a large cage, big enough for them to flap their wings and fly. He had been rewarded by an annual nest, a crude affair constructed from a few rough twigs, and an occasional egg, which both parents invariably ignored. But this year it was different. The vultures were doing their best to sit on the uncomfortable nest, and eventually they hatched a chick.

As ugly as its parents, but covered in grey down instead of black feathers, the infant hopped on its ungainly legs, to the delight of Mott and other enthusiastic naturalists. It was the first Griffon vulture ever to be hatched in captivity and Chester Zoo was beginning to make a name for breeding 'difficult' species. The baby grew to maturity and still enjoys good health in the zoo.

When visiting zoologists seek reasons to explain the phenomenon, Mr Mottershead points out that he did nothing more than give the birds room in which to move naturally, fresh air and sunlight, and sufficient 'props', such as tree trunks and branches, to provide interest. Given these basic ingredients, nature takes over and does the rest. Hundreds of years of total restraint had resulted in feeble, bored creatures that had no incentive either to prolong their own lives or to propagate the species.

At three o'clock one morning there was an urgent telephone call to say that Bristol had been badly bombed and a direct hit had damaged the zoo. Would Chester accept four lions as it was unsafe to let them remain in their own zoo?

Mott and his keepers began adapting more of the stables in readiness for the lions which arrived later that day. They could not be housed with the resident animals and had to have their own quarters. Surprisingly, the bombing did not seem to have worried them, and they were none the worse for their long journey. Their enclosure was not as big as it ought to have been, Mott felt, but it was as big as, if not bigger, than those at other zoos.

With so many lions about the place and so many dens to be kept scrupulously clean, Mott was delighted to welcome a London woman who had been evacuated to Chester and who had come seeking work with animals. She was quite unafraid of lions and readily accepted responsibility. Mott appointed a fourten-year-old boy as her assistant and together they looked after the colony of lions.

The females were breeding and one, Cassandra, the daughter of Patrick and Faith, had been bred in Chester and was now expecting her first litter. The boy was helping to clean out the dens one day when he opened the inner den-gate without first closing the outer one. In a bound, three lionesses leapt through the gate and were free in the zoo gardens. Mott heard the shout of alarm and went to investigate. The boy stood petrified, expecting the lions to spring at him at any moment.

'Go into the house,' Mott told him briefly. Lions can smell fear and it can trigger off an attack. He fetched hunks of meat and threw them into the den, then stood back to watch. Two of the lionesses came trotting up and walked right back into their enclosure, but the third, Cassandra, who was due to cub any day, was nowhere to be seen.

Mott walked softly and slowly this way and that, looking for the flick of a bush that might betray the animal's presence. He was reluctant to get his gun. Cassandra was a valuable lioness, and her cubs would help to wipe out some of the deficit. Besides, he had never had to shoot one of his animals yet.

While the keepers watched from the house windows, Mott stalked round the garden peering into every clump of bushes. Cassandra saw him coming and tried to shrink deeper into the mass of azaleas that were hiding her. She backed away from him, crouching low to the ground, her claws extended and her nose wrinkling into a snarl. From the corner of her eye she could see the open door to her enclosure, the other lionesses having been securely fastened into their inner den. She ran straight back into her cage, while Mott followed and locked the door. One hour later she gave birth to six healthy cubs, a performance she was to repeat at regular intervals for the rest of her life, making Mott eternally grateful that he had used gentle methods of recapturing her after her brief bid for freedom.

Not only wild animals sought shelter at Chester Zoo. Frequent requests came from owners of monkeys and delicate pets who found wartime shortages more than they had bargained for. But the zoo could not take on such liabilities and had to refuse, reluctant though it was to limit its stock. One animal that was accepted, though, was Ben, an outsize St Bernard that was eating its master out of house and home.

Ben would have taken no prizes as a guard dog. The courtyard, with its strange noises, the roars and squeaks of assorted inmates, gave him nightmares, and he preferred to use the front door of the house and give the creatures a wide berth. Nevertheless he looked fierce and as June was feeling lonely now that Muriel had joined the WRNs, he made a fine and gentle pet.

There was a heavy snowfall one night and early the next morning, soon after first light, the alarm sounded at the zoo. A lion had escaped. Mott and his keepers tore round the cages taking stock of the animals. Not one was missing. But reports kept coming in from the surrounding district that a wild animal, perhaps a tiger, was at large.

Mystified, Mott went to the village himself to see the traces. They were giant paw marks, leading straight out of the zoo's main gate and down the lane where they were lost in a maze of other marks. They seemed big enough to have been made by a lion, but then Ben was just about the same size! He had to be walked round the district so that everyone could see the culprit.

The lean years of work and worry paid off, and 1942 was a red-letter year. Instead of the usual deficit, there was a profit of £467, the first the Society had ever made. Mrs Mottershead and June were run off their feet some weekends when the café and refreshment room in the big house did a roaring trade. Many new visitors were those who had 'adopted' animals which they came to see, but a few were regulars who had watched the zoo grow.

Miss Tompkyns-Grafton made the journey from the Lake District to Chester several times each year to follow Punch's progress and she never became reconciled to his disreputable appearance. Early in 1944 when his quarters needed a considerable amount of repair, Mott put forward an alternative scheme to the Ministry when he had to apply for a licence. Instead of patching up the old den, he asked, why not build an entirely new enclosure with no bars and therefore with no necessity for metal which was becoming extremely scarce?

The Ministry granted permission, and Mott began his herculean labour of mixing tons of cement and sand and creating a bear plateau surrounded by a deep ditch and a stout wall. Before he began, Miss Tompkyns-Grafton asked him about his design and enquired if it would be possible to incorporate a large pool. As expense was the only hitch, she offered to pay the cost of building a pool. Mott was delighted. He had long realised that his polar bear enclosure was far from ideal, but so were many things in the zoo, including the lives he and his wife were leading, with so much work and so little leisure.

It was a mammoth task and it took all winter to build. Then 30,000 gallons of clear water were pumped into the pool and Punch and Judy transferred to their new quarters. Mott stood back waiting for the splash. Judy rolled into the water in ecstasy, but Punch was not interested.

Mott's heart sank. He had telephoned Miss Tompkyns-Grafton as he had promised to let her know that the work was finished. Now she had come to Chester and he was to call for her at her hotel at eight o'clock the next morning. She preferred to arrive at the zoo very early so that she could spend most of the day there.

Before he drove into Chester the next morning, Mott went to the bears to see if Punch had had a secret bath. But he was just as filthy as he had always been. All the way to the zoo Miss Tompkyns-Grafton kept asking questions about the pool and how Punch liked it. Mott made brief and noncommittal answers. He had not the heart to tell her the truth. He felt thoroughly ashamed of his bear, and dreaded seeing the old lady's disappointment.

It was a damp day and they had to trudge through a patch of mud before they reached the bear's enclosure.

Both animals were sitting side by side on the plateau watching their approach, and Mott dropped a step or so behind. He did not want to see his companion's expression.

She leaned over the wall and called, in her clear, precise voice, 'Now come along, you two! Let me see how you like your new home.'

The very next second both bears shambled to the edge of the pool and slid in, churning up the crystal clear water so that it became the texture and colour of pea soup. Mott stared in disbelief as Punch cavorted in the water, the dirt rolling off him like black lather.

Miss Tompkyns-Grafton did not stay long, and on the drive back to Chester she broke her silence.

'I can die in peace, now that Punch has had a bath,' she said. 'Thank you for all you have done for him.'

She died later the same year, leaving £18,000 to the zoo, a legacy that was to lift the Society out of the red and set its course for future expansion. All debts were paid, mortgages and debentures cleared, and forty acres of land adjoining the zoo were bought for future extensions. Without the heavy halter of debt round his neck, Mott was able to concentrate more on animals and less on finance. The pride of lions had gone from strength to strength, breeding eighty-four cubs. Some had been sold to new zoos springing up towards the end of the war, and now more had to go. Chester was overrun with lions and they had become so scarce (none having been imported from Africa during the war) that Mott was getting up to a hundred pounds for each lion. It was like a vein of gold and he mined it fully, setting aside reserves with which to buy new animals once the war was over and overseas trading became possible. Later he was to export his home grown lions to African zoos, many of which had run out of exhibits.

By the time the war ended, only one animal had died

as a result of enemy action—a coypu rat that had been neatly beheaded by a piece of shrapnel. But the gardens had been neglected for lack of labour and money, and many of the pens and enclosures were in urgent need of repair.

The conservatory, which had accommodated birds, snakes and alligators, had been so badly damaged by blast and shrapnel that it was beyond repair. The birds had been moved into the courtyard and the reptiles into the basement aquarium where June struggled manfully, often against overwhelming odds. Whenever it rained heavily she was ankle deep in water, and cleaning out the tanks meant swilling the contents on to the floor, then brushing this out into the drains.

Fortunately the two alligators, now five feet long, could be persuaded to do anything for her so long as she gave their backs a good brushing with a broom kept for that purpose. They would open their mouths, close their eyes, and all but purr with pleasure.

The lizards were quite another matter. One species would pretend to be asleep, then, when she leaned into their tank to clean the glass, they would lash out with their tails, leaving angry red weals on her cheek. A viper caused a crisis when it gave birth to a large number of babies during the night. They swarmed away from their mother and made their way upstairs to the restaurant. Mrs Mottershead discovered them before any visitors had arrived, and everyone joined in the hunt to recapture the poisonous infants before any harm was done.

But the most pressing need was for a bigger lion enclosure. The time had come for Mott to try out his experiment of letting his lions return to nature. A new Council had been elected, this time of only fifteen members, and they all agreed to give the scheme a trial.

The area chosen, close to the big house, contained a small copse of tall trees, sufficient to give shade but with no low overhanging branches to facilitate escape, and the strongest chain-link fencing on the market was erected to a height of twelve feet, with a two-foot inward overhang at the top. In addition, a three-foot high fence was erected round the outside to discourage the public from putting their fingers through the wire.

It was with some trepidation that the Council met one morning to see the lions being turned loose in the pasture. The young ones gambolled on the grass but their elders clung together, lashing their tails and pressing back their ears, as if afraid of the large open space. They sniffed the grass with suspicion, then walked stiff-legged round the perimeter snarling at the trees and the posts that supported the wire. The males settled down first, leaving the females to continue the prowl, and it was almost a week before they began to forget they had lived elsewhere.

Some members of the public, together with many zoologists, condemned the enclosure, saying it was unsafe and not warm enough for the animals. In fact, the lions had an enclosed den at the rear where they could go if they felt cold, but they seldom did, even when snow was on the ground.

The lions became remarkably hardy, much healthier, and bred without any encouragement. As for their escaping, not one ever got out. Years later (in 1966) Mr Mottershead was invited by the Wiltshire County Council to come as an independent witness and advise whether the wire fence being erected round Longleat, the home of the Marquis of Bath, was sufficiently strong to withstand lions. It was stronger that that at Chester Zoo and Mr Mottershead was able to convince the councillors of its safety.

Whenever he had a free moment he would watch the lions enjoying their freedom. At times the pride consisted of three or four males and half a dozen females and cubs. The males gave the impression of being the masters, but his observations taught Mott the opposite. Several times he watched fierce battles when two or three males would spring at each other with bared teeth and unsheathed claws. At first he was inclined to interfere and stop the fight, but he resisted. The lions would make a tremendous noise, bringing people from all parts of the zoo to 'Ooh' and 'Aah' as they tussled and struggled as if in mortal combat. The females would take little interest for a while, then a lioness would stalk up to the fighters, land a clout on their heads with the flat of a paw, and stand waving her tail until the combatants backed away from each other and peace reigned again. There was no doubt who was really the boss in the world of lions.

A tiger enclosure built on the same lines, only smaller, was not quite ready when the first tiger arrived, so he was installed in the old lion den with sheer walls twelve feet high and a glass skylight in the roof. He seemed to settle down for the night, and early the next morning Mott went to see if he was all right. He was shocked to find the den empty, the tiger gone. A closer inspection revealed splinters of glass on the floor and the skylight window broken.

Mott sounded the alarm to call the keepers who had already begun work, then he telephoned the police. No one knew better than he the savagery that could result if the tiger were not caught—or shot—immediately. Fortunately it was too early for visitors, but the zoo gates were locked as a precaution. Keepers were told to search every bush, every outhouse and building, while Mott armed himself with a gun and joined in the search.

It was nerve-racking work. They skirted clumps of bushes, half-expecting that the tiger would leap out at them any moment. Then there was a shout. Someone had found a paw print. Mott told the others to stand

55

back while he followed the tracks, his gun at the ready. They led round the lion enclosure to where there was a narrow passage between it and the building. When he reached the corner he paused, for there was the tiger pressed up against the fencing, snarling softly at a lioness inside. His fur glistened in the sunlight and Mott thought he had never seen such a beautiful animal. He put away his gun and crept back to the keepers.

'Go and get all the wire netting you can find,' he told them. 'Be as quiet and as quick as you can, and with a bit of luck we'll catch him alive. Now hurry.'

Working fast and silently, they blocked both ends of the passage with wire netting, then one keeper climbed on to the roof of the building and rolled a length of wire along the top, enclosing the tiger in the alley. It was a simple task then to entice the lionesses into their den and lock them in so that Mott could go into the lion enclosure with a trap cage and a pair of wire cutters. He cut a large hole in the fence, placed the trap against it, and gave the word for the keepers to bang on the wire to frighten the tiger into the trap. It worked as planned and the animal was recaptured, none the worse for its adventure.

For some time Mott felt uneasy about the tiger enclosure, but he need not have worried for none of them ever got out. Some years later a great elm tree crashed on to the perimeter fence during a storm, bringing it down and making a gangway over which the tigers could have walked to freedom. Instead, they sniffed suspiciously and snarled loud and long until a keeper came to investigate the disturbance and repair the damage. It is an accepted fact by many of the keepers at Chester Zoo that the animals are not keen to be set free, and prefer the protection that wire gives them.

One exception was Ferdinand, an enormous bison that had spent the best part of his life behind bars.

When he found himself in a paddock surrounded only by a low fence and a ditch, he promptly leapt over it and went for a walk round the grounds. As it happened there were no visitors about and Mott, helped by his daughter and his wife, coaxed and cajoled him back into captivity. Such bids for freedom had been anticipated and Mr Mottershead decided to use Ferdie as a guinea pig to try out methods, other than bars, of keeping him penned in. He fixed a low voltage electric wire round the fence and stood back ready to switch off the current if it proved too much for the bison.

Ferdie had watched the preparations with great interest and now he thudded over to the wire and licked it. He tossed his great head and pawed the ground—then went back to the wire and licked it again. Each time he felt the tingling shock he shrugged his hump and shook his head, but there was no doubt about it, electricity tasted fine to Ferdie.

Mott went back to the house to work out a new plan, and behind him followed Ferdie, tired of the wire, but ever eager for new treats from his master.

As more visitors came, Ferdie learned to stay captive just as long as strangers were about. But as soon as the last visitor had gone, he would leap over his fence and make for the front lawn where he slept each night. Years later he taught his infant son the same tricks, but they both played fair and pretended to be captive during working hours.

Escapes were not always so funny. During a particularly heavy snowfall, a large Malayan bear noted for its bad temper walked to freedom when snow drifted into the ditch surrounding its enclosure. The first anyone knew of it was when Mott's secretary, who lived in the big house with other members of the staff, heard something scratching on the front door. She was expecting her boy-friend to call for her, and thought he was playing a trick on her.

Deciding to turn the tables on him, she put out the hall light and went to the open front door. In walked the huge shambling bear. Mr and Mrs Mottershead heard her scream from their living room upstairs, and ran down at once. The bear was pacing angrily in the hall and Mott told his secretary to keep away from it while he went to get a large crate. He handed her a bag of sweets with which to pacify it, but told her to take no chances.

Getting the crate was not as easy as it sounded, for snowdrifts had piled up against all the outbuildings and the doors had to be dug out before they could be opened. While Mott and a keeper were thus occupied, the secretary had lost her fear of the bear, for it was sitting on its haunches like an overgrown puppy, begging for sweets. Enchanted, she gave it the lot, when it stopped being cuddly and became its old menacing self.

When there were no more sweets forthcoming, the bear turned its attention to the furniture. Chairs and tables went flying, then it began on the oak panelling, digging its claws in as though it were butter and leaving scars that remain to this day. The noise of Mott arriving at the back door disturbed it. It clambered up to a mullioned window and hurled itself through the glass, landing in the snow unhurt, but even more savage.

Mott went to get his gun and began a desperate hunt in the dark. Paths had been cut in the deep snow and, where they intersected, Mott slowed his steps, his gun raised. There was no sound other than the crunch of snow beneath his feet and his heavy breathing. Suddenly a shadow ahead took shape and lumbered towards him. It was the bear, only a short distance from the main gate and freedom. With a heavy heart Mott lifted his gun, took aim, and fired, killing the bear instantly. The risk of trying to capture it alive against such overwhelming odds could not be considered.

Mrs Mottershead had a private contretemps with a Himalayan bear, but with a happier outcome. It had escaped from its den by climbing up a sheer wall and had spent an hour roaming round the zoo. June and a keeper cornered it and were coaxing it back to its quarters when Mrs Mottershead came out to praise it for coming quietly. She walked right up to it to give it a piece of bread, when it struck her down and pounced upon her, sinking its claws into her flesh. The keeper grabbed a pitchfork and was prepared to fight to the death, but the bear capitulated at once and ran back to its den of its own accord.

June telephoned the doctor, then got the whisky bottle. Her mother did not want any—she was wonderfully resilient and was already excusing the bear's behaviour and blaming herself for having startled it. But June was shaken to the core by the narrow escape. Mother needed anti-tetanus injections and dressings for her wounds, while June was given aspirin to cure her hangover next day.

CHAPTER SEVEN

CHIMPANZEES' ISLAND

When Fred Williams came looking for a job as a keeper at Chester Zoo after he was demobbed from the RAF in 1946, he had never been face to face with anything more ferocious than a guinea pig. But he loved animals, had kept them as pets all his life, and now wanted to work with them. The zoo was expanding rapidly, swapping lion cubs for all sorts of other animals, and Fred had to turn his hand to a variety of jobs. Soon after his arrival news came that two sealions were on their way from California. The pool that had been planned for them was not yet finished, and the only place with sufficient water for them was a bear pit with a 30,000-gallon pool.

Sammy and Susie were year-old pups; he weighed about ninety pounds and she was a little lighter. He was one of the most aggressive sealions ever to be captured. Right from the start he liked Fred, but the first week he was at Chester he took a violent dislike to a press photographer and went for him, nipping his knee and flinging him to the ground. Susie used to bark for help when Sammy began knocking her about and Fred frequently intervened and persuaded Sammy to be less boisterous.

Their cement-lined pool had steeply sloping sides, slippery with algae, but the sealions could cling to it like limpets. Fred went in with a bucket of fish to feed them each day, and because they would not let him leave until they were certain that he had no more fish, it became his habit to dip the pail into the pool, haul it out and pour away the water. Only then would the sealions allow him to leave. One day, however, Fred must have dipped the bucket in too deep, for instead of his lifting it out, it pulled him down the slippery sides of the pool. In an instant his wellington boots filled with water, and he swam furiously against his ever-increasing weight, trying to gain a foothold on the slope.

Sammy and Susie were delighted with this new game, and they circled him, dipping and diving, watching what he would do next. It was bitterly cold and there was not a soul in sight to answer his shouts for help. He struck out for the far side of the pool where there was a concrete ledge projecting above the water, and after a hard struggle, he managed to pull himself out.

Soon afterwards a bulldozer was hired to scoop out a large pond as a permanent home for the sealions. This time it was surrounded by a grassy border and a stout waist-high railing. It succeeded in keeping people out, but it was never a real barrier to keep the animals in. On the first day Susie was taken to her new enclosure, she flipped over the railings and returned to her own pool. And whenever Sammy was rough with her, she would take off in search of a keeper, complaining loudly all the way.

Susie's habits probably prolonged her life, for in subsequent years Sammy's amorous attacks killed several of his wives. Post-mortem examinations showed he had made deep bites, probably in affection, but nevertheless fatal. And when one wife managed to rear a live cub, Sammy was so keen to teach it to swim that he killed it in play.

For all his roughness with his harem, Sammy was invariably gentle with his keepers. When he was fully grown, he weighed over six hundred pounds and had a voice that could be heard a mile away. He seldom went for a walk when visitors were about, preferring the safety of his enclosure, but when the main gates had been locked in the evening, he sometimes went in search of a change of scene. Usually he made his own way home before dark, and if he went near the other animals they would beat on their doors and raise their voices to let the keepers know that something was amiss. Sammy's insatiable greed for herrings made him an obedient animal, and he would follow Fred anywhere in return for a bonus fish.

As Chester Zoo grew, people from far afield wrote asking for advice on how to keep their pets and sometimes, when they outgrew their homes, the animals would be presented to the zoo. Such an animal was One-Lung, a Himalayan bear with a wicked temper. Her owner had reared her from a cub but now she was too big; as her owner had only one lung (hence the bear's name) he did not feel able to cope with her any longer.

She was introduced to the colony of Russian, Canadian and Himalayan bears and soon settled down. She formed a particular attachment to Trotski, a Russian bear, and surprised everyone some months later when it became obvious that she was pregnant. Mothers and cubs cannot be left to live in the colony but have to be segregated, which meant that One-Lung was left in charge of the enclosure and the others were transferred to the only spare den. This was really too small for so many assorted bears, but it was the only way. Although the zoo was slightly more affluent than it had been, every penny had to be counted and there was nothing to spare for new bear pits.

Fred looked after One-Lung, giving her extra vitamins and rations. One morning he caught sight of two tiny cubs, not much bigger than kittens, before she moved them to the back of her sleeping quarters. Fred could tell they were well by the constant buzzing sound they made, almost like a hive of bees. Day by day the buzzing grew louder. Then one day it was much fainter. One of the cubs had obviously died, probably accidentally crushed by its mother. The other survived though, and when it was three or four months old, it came into the open.

After a few days, when the cub was used to playing outside, Fred and another keeper enticed One-Lung into her sleeping den and dropped the iron-barred trap door, locking her in while they entered the outdoor enclosure to examine the cub and discover its sex. Although it was no bigger than a small dog, it stood on its hind legs and snarled at them, prepared to do battle. One-Lung was in a fury, crashing her seven hundred-or-so pounds against the gate in such a way that it seemed she would burst it open. It was of the strongest iron, but it had never been subjected to a strain such as this and the keepers raced round after the little bear, doing their best to catch it so that they could make their escape. When they did finally corner the cub, the keeper who was more experienced than Fred examined it and said it was a female.

The cub was named 'Belinda' and handed back to her mother, none the worse for her adventure. Meanwhile the other bears were growing restless with their long confinement in smaller quarters, and it was decided that they must be returned to their own den. But Belinda had to be removed. She no longer needed her mother, and she became Fred's responsibility.

She had a large cage and each day, when he was not too busy, Fred got in with her and had a rough and tumble. As she grew older and much bigger, she could knock him down with one affectionate swipe of a paw, and he had to call a halt to the play before he was hurt. Instead, he slipped a chain round her neck and took her for walks round the zoo as he went about his jobs. A fig tree grew against the wall facing her cage and she loved to climb up it and look out over the neighbourhood, but she always came trotting back when called.

In the cage next to hers were two monkeys with whom she was great friends. They learnt how to put their paws through the wire and slide back the bolt on Belinda's door. She would then push it open and go for a walk. A padlock soon stopped this game, but whenever Fred had unlocked the padlock preparatory to going in to clean the cage, the monkeys would slide back the bolt and jump with excitement as Belinda walked out.

When she had been on her own for about a year, it was decided that she was big enough, at five feet high, to fend for herself, and that she should now join the other bears in the colony. Fred hated to part with her; she was so tame and intelligent that he felt he could have trained her to do all manner of tricks. But it was pointed out to him that this was a zoo, not a circus, and that animals must be allowed to live with their own kind and not as human pets. Meanwhile it was found that the keeper who had determined the bear's sex had made a mistake: it was a male, but the name Belinda stuck.

Fred was given the job of transferring him to the bears' enclosure and thought it would be a simple matter of walking Belinda straight there instead of going the other way, as they had done together so often. But he had forgotten about the animal pens that bordered the path leading to the bears' enclosure. Belinda trotted along beside him, the chain around his neck, until he caught the tigers' scent. Immediately he jerked to his six-foot height, felled Fred with one paw, and lumbered away at top speed.

As soon as he picked himself up, Fred gave chase, and found Belinda up the fig tree, growling and grumbling and begging to go back to his own cage. This time Fred put the bear in a crate and wheeled him to the other bears. He watched anxiously as Belinda joined the colony. Now he was alongside his mother, it was obvious that he was not pure Himalayan, but half Russian. This became even more apparent when he attained his full height, a magnificent six feet, towering over the Himalayan bears, and with thick black fur of an entirely different texture. As if he sensed his ancestry, he chose to throw in his lot with the Russian bears. But he never forgot his nursery companion. When Fred paused, as he did each day, to see how the bears were getting on, Belinda would gaze back and stand on his hindlegs, watching until Fred was out of sight. If Fred called 'Belinda', the bear would halt in his tracks and hesitate, perhaps trying to recall the companionship of youth. But the decision had been made in time. Belinda was not too humanised, and was able to take his place in the bear world with hardly a backward glance.

Sometimes keepers can fill a desperate, though temporary, need. Wally was one of four black-footed penguins that lived as remotely as possible from humans. So long as they were fed on time, they had not a thought for their providers. Then one night a fox raided their enclosure and killed three of the penguins, leaving only Wally alive. He waddled up to Fred as soon as he arrived next morning, beside himself with distress, climbed on to Fred's boots and beat a tattoo with his flippers. He had to be stroked and soothed before he would eat and then, to take his mind off his ordeal, Fred picked him out of his pen and let him amble along beside him as he did his rounds of the zoo. After that there was no keeping Wally penned up. Wherever Fred went, Wally had to go too, except when there were visitors about and the penguins, like most of the other animals, seemed to realise that things were different during working hours. But apart from weekends, most days were very quiet so early in the year, and Wally had the freedom of the zoo.

Among his other chores, Fred did repairs to the plumbing, electrical fittings and buildings. One day he was on top of a ladder in the reptile house repairing a section of the wiring, when he became aware, from the corner of his eye, of something moving beneath him. It was Wally, doing his best to climb up the ladder. On Whit Monday when hundreds of people gave the zoo the best 'gate' it had ever had, Wally manfully stayed in his pen, but his keen eyes had picked out Fred down the drive and people crowded to watch the solitary penguin dance and cry out, running this way and that, trying to watch Fred's movements about the zoo.

It was tiring having a penguin for a shadow, but it ended abruptly the day some new penguins arrived. Wally welcomed them wholeheartedly and although he still went to greet Fred at feeding time, he never tried to follow him again now that he had companions of his own breed.

Animals, visitors and problems multiplied alarmingly towards the end of the 1940s with the ever-increasing prestige of Chester Zoo. While certain animals were still extremely rare—and expensive—Mr Mottershead was often given first refusal. An English doctor and his wife in Sierra Leone had five baby chimpanzees that were getting too big to be kept as pets. The doctor's father lived in Lymm, Cheshire, and had spoken highly of Chester Zoo. Now the doctor wrote to Mott asking if he would like to have the chimps. Would he! Although he was running short of space, he could not bear to turn away such an opportunity. He wrote immediately and arangements were made to have the animals despatched.

Elmer, Solomon, Simon, Meg and Babu were installed in a large cage in the monkey house where, for the time being, they settled down without any trouble.

Word came from London that three giraffes had arrived and would be coming to Chester as soon as they had served their term in quarantine. The zoo had never had a giraffe, and had no building that could possibly be adapted. Mott and Fred examined ways and means of building a large enough house. The first requirement had to be the animals' comfort; only when this was satisfied could aesthetic appeal be considered. To make matters worse, all building materials were scarce and costly.

For some time Mr Mottershead had been using sandstone, which he could get fairly easily, and he had bought several tons of ex-War Department steel tubes. He decided that these tubes could be welded together to form the skeleton of the roof, but the problem was how to raise such a prefabricated structure to the top of the walls. He came up with the idea of using jacks, similar to those used when changing car wheels. The gigantic span of roof was put together and welded on the floor to the exact measurements required. Jacks were put under each truss along one side and raised eighteen inches. It was slow, tedious work, building the wall a foot and a half at a time so that the jacks could be removed and taken to the other side of the roof where the whole performance began again. Inch by inch the mammoth roof was raised into position, the only scaffolding being the framework round the walls over which the men scrambled as they carried the jacks backwards and forwards. When it was finished, it was forty feet high, spacious enough for even the longest-necked giraffe.

Meanwhile Fred had married June Mottershead and they spent their evenings first planning, then building a new aquarium. The old one in the basement of Oakfield was becoming impossible. June had been in charge of it since the end of the war and conditions were getting worse each year. Whenever it rained the aquarium flooded and had to be pumped out and, in addition, the presence of so much water was making the whole house damp.

During their holidays, June and Fred visited every known aquarium in Britain, studying the various plans and buildings, deciding which points they would and would not incorporate in their design. Together they drew up plans for what constituted their ideal, bearing in mind Mott's dogma—'make everything much bigger than at first seems necessary, give the creatures room to move, and provide natural vegetation.' The plans were submitted first to Mr Mottershead and then to the Zoo Council, and were passed with the proviso that no workmen could be recruited specially, so the aquarium could not be built until the staff had time to fit it in.

June was not her father's daughter for nothing; she had been taught to take impossibilities in her stride right from infancy and now she was able to put her training to use.

Every night when the last visitor had gone, June and Fred changed into overalls and set about building the aquarium themselves. Mott managed to buy cheaply two aircraft runway landing lights at an army surplus sale, and these were rigged up to provide illumination. The building was to be made of concrete pillars, each six inches by six inches by ten feet six inches high. Between them, June and Fred managed to cast two pillars every evening until they had made the requisite one hundred and thirty. Then they laid a six-inch-thick concrete foundation, leaving a square hole for each post.

It was slow, boring, and often heavy work: setting the posts, filling in the framework first with wire, then expanded metal, and finally sand-lime cement mortar. It took the best part of two years. Problems begot problems. The exceptionally large tropical tanks needed an unforeseen amount of heating pipes which were just not available. Some other means of heating had to be found. They decided to use a heating cable consisting of an element enclosed in a copper jacket. Several of these were passed through the tanks, to the consternation of many who thought the copper might kill the fish. It was a calculated risk—and it paid off. The fish thrived and this method of heating was so efficient that it was made permanent and was even used in new tanks long after the more conservative heating pipes had become available.

An attractive feature of the new aquarium was a roof tank encircling the building. It was three feet wide, fifteen inches deep and two hundred and forty feet long. Glass panels were set in the bottom of the tank so that people inside the aquarium building could look up and see fish swimming overhead. This tank also supplied filtered water to the tanks below. For some time the zoo had bred quantities of goldfish in the moat round the bear pits, and when the aquarium was finished and ready to be opened, June and Fred caught all these fish and installed them in the roof tank. It was hard work moving seven hundred goldfish, and when they had finished they went for lunch.

They had hardly started when a gardener rushed in, begging them to hurry as it was raining goldfish! The roof of the aquarium must have attracted every seagull from miles around. They were swooping and screaming, snatching fish and letting them fall on the heads of bewildered visitors who found themselves being bombarded with squirming goldfish. June, Fred and every available helper rushed about with jars and tins trying to rescue the castaways, but from the original seven hundred only forty were saved. After that, only fish larger than trout were kept in the roof tank and it was covered with wire netting as an extra precaution. Eventually it was found to be more trouble than it was worth and the tank was converted into a roof garden.

Developing the zoo was frequently as precarious as walking a tight-rope blindfold. An ill-considered action could not only harm the animals, but seriously upset the delicate balance between profit and loss. During the nineteen-forties zoos were springing up all over Britain and, in fact, the world, but there was little contact between them. True, they wrote to each other, trading and selling their stock, but they were not able to compare notes and share experiences.

In 1949 an old friend of Mr Mottershead's, Cedric Flood of Dublin Zoo, suggested forming an association of British and Irish zoos which could hold annual conferences where the directors would be able to exchange ideas. Mott joined immediately and the first conference was held at Dublin Zoo, the second at Chester. At about the same time, directors of zoos in other parts of the world felt the same need of mutual help and they formed the International Union of Directors of Zoological Gardens. Both bodies were to help enormously in the future development of world zoos, but those that benefited most were the animals in captivity.

While his lions and tigers were enjoying unprecedented freedom and proving their contentment by breeding freely, Mott was not satisfied with his birds and chimps. For some time he had toyed with the idea of building an enclosed jungle, a huge structure in which tropical trees and plants could grow in profusion, making a natural home where birds of different species would build their own nests. It was a grandiose scheme which had to remain a dream until the zoo's finances were considerably more healthy. It was to cost £100,000 and become the finest tropical house in the world. While to everyone else it seemed like wishing for the moon, to George Mottershead it was a necessity if he were to keep faith in his ideals and free captive creatures.

He made a six-foot model representing a two-hundred-foot square building bordered on one side by a nocturnal house, on another by a reptile house and on another by an ape house.

Frequently he was brought back to earth by the need for larger premises for the chimpanzees, all five of which had not only thrived, but had grown so strong in both wind and limb that they were rapidly reducing their quarters to ruins. In the beginning they had had plenty of room to move in the huge cage they shared in the monkey house. But as they grew, they tested their strength against the fabric of their home. Elmer, the largest, loved nothing better than to take hold of the iron-barred door and shake it with increasing force until it came out of its fastenings. He was an amiable, docile animal and on the best possible terms with his keeper, but Mott realised that the healthy chimps needed something more than a cage to engage their attentions. Little by little the walls developed cracks. Showers of plaster rained down on both chimps and visitors alike, and life became a battle of wits between the animals and their keepers.

Mr Mottershead was reluctant to strengthen their cage, or even build a bigger one, without first investigating possible ways to confine them with greater freedom. Frequently foreign zoologists were coming to

Chester, having heard of its *avant-garde* ideas that, to their surprise, actually worked. To each Mott put his question: was there some way, other than bars, to contain chimpanzees? But nobody had any suggestions.

While the problem was pigeon-holed at the back of his mind, George Mottershead turned his attention to yet another urgent necessity—a means of transport about the zoo. Many more acres had been added, the gardens had been planned to set off the animal enclosures, and members of the public were having to walk long distances if they were to see all the exhibits. Other zoos had various means of internal transport ranging from small buses to equally small railway systems, but he disliked them all. For one thing they were too noisy; for another, they interfered with the enjoyment of families who could stroll along paths untroubled by danger of traffic.

Delighted with his hire of the bulldozer that had made such short work of scooping out the sealions' pool, Mr Mottershead decided to buy one. It was a wonderful investment, for it inspired him to plan a network of waterways through, and round, the zoo. The earth dug out was banked to form hills and dales and, in some cases, islands inside lakes. It was one of these islands, designed for waterfowl, that suggested a solution to the chimp problem. Mott eagerly looked through reference books to see what the authorities had to say about chimpanzees and water. Information was singularly lacking. Some experts considered that chimps could not swim and therefore would never venture near water, but others maintained it was lack of opportunity and familiarity that bred the fear, and that animals as intelligent as these would soon come to terms with water.

On his visits to other zoos in Europe, Mott looked for proof and found none. Other zoo directors whom he met at annual conferences looked askance when he put forward his ideas of creating island homes for chimps with no bars to keep them in. But then, he consoled himself, people were still shaking their heads and wondering by what magic Chester lions were persuaded to keep behind their wire netting when the rest of the world's captive lions required iron bars.

In 1956 Mr Mottershead went to Chicago to the International Conference and asked directors from zoos all over the world if they had had experience of a chimp trying to swim. The answer was no, qualified by the fact that in most zoos chimps never came face to face with water except what they saw in their drinking dishes.

The time had come for action. Shortly before he had left for America, Mott had had an example of what to expect if the chimps were not rehoused quickly. The zoo had acquired two new chimpanzees, four-year-olds that had been in a circus. On their first night at Chester they were installed in a cage next to the resident five in the monkey house, and they all seemed to settle down very well. But a few nights later when a keeper was doing her evening rounds, she heard a commotion from the chimps and went to investigate. The resident five were leaping round their cage excitedly, and the other cage was empty. Boden and Prince, the newcomers, had broken down a door leading to the storeroom behind, where their food was kept. The keeper ran to raise the alarm. There was no question of forcing the chimps back into their cage—they were already powerful animals quite capable of doing serious injury if thwarted. Mott and two keepers hid in the passage adjoining the storeroom and kept watch while Boden switched on the electric stove, poured some cocoa into a pan of milk and tried to heat it. Prince found an opened tin of condensed milk and a jar of malt and after eating some of each, poured the rest in a keeper's trilby hat that was hanging behind the door. Only when the chimps were showing signs of boredom were they approached by Mr Mottershead. He led them back to their cage, to which a new door had meanwhile been fitted.

If two strange chimps could break out, then it was only goodwill that was keeping the resident five in.

Keeping in mind the tropical house of the future, Mott had an apehouse constructed in such a way that it could form one side of the house when, if ever, it was built. The apehouse was alongside an artificial lake in which there was a series of islands. Each was in the shape of a peninsula with the isthmus leading to an indoor den. In this way separate families of chimps could inhabit their own islands, have their own indoor quarters and live almost side by side with other colonies without the need to fight and defend their territories. The islands were separated from each other by water and surrounded by a moat cutting them off from a path along which visitors could walk.

The dens were large rooms which had armour-plated glass windows instead of bars or fencing. For years Mr Mottershead and other zoo directors had been aware that many chimps and monkeys were susceptible to human ailments, particularly respiratory infections, and each year many died from pneumonia and tuberculosis. It had long been accepted that these germs were introduced to the animals through the bars. Now he was killing two birds with one stone; he was freeing the chimps from their cages and also from the source of much infection.

The chimps were transferred to their islands on a quiet day when there were few visitors, and all keepers were warned to be prepared for an escape. Chattering to themselves at the strangeness of it all, the chimps explored their surroundings, keeping close to each other until they gained confidence. Solomon was the first to go near the water, and everyone held their breath. He looked down at his reflection, and jumped back in alarm. He went back and peered closer, jabbing a finger at the stranger reflected in the water. Shaking his wet fist, he stamped on the ground and backed rapidly away from the water's edge. The keepers relaxed their guard. It was obvious that chimpanzees did not like water.

Once they settled down on the islands, the chimps began to look around, and found various stones and half bricks left behind by the builders. It didn't take them long to recognise the stones as missiles to be flung at visitors who stood in the public passage of the apehouse looking out on the islands through armour-plated glass windows. Many of the stones hit glass strong enough to withstand the onslaught. But one brick hit the glass in a vital spot and the pane disintegrated, leaving an escape route for the chimps. Solomon and Elmer climbed through first, closely followed by Meg, Simon and Babu. The last three went on to the roof, content to sit there surveying the scene, but Solomon and Elmer made off for the zebra paddock where they had the time of their lives chasing the zebras from one end of the field to the other.

Once the alarm was raised, keepers soon coaxed the three on the roof back into their den. Solomon came when called and allowed himself to be taken inside, but Elmer evaded the keeper and jumped on to the roof of the apehouse. Fred Williams had been syringing flowers nearby and he called to Elmer, waving the syringe at him. It was a gesture that nearly cost him his life, for Elmer interpreted it as a threat. He sprang down, landing just behind Fred, seized his jacket with one huge first, and then began raining blows on his back. When a three-hundred-pound chimpanzee launches an attack, there is only one thing to do—run. And Fred ran as he had never run before, with Elmer tearing along after him, landing heavy blows, any one of which could have broken Fred's spine had it landed on his back.

Fred ran towards the lake, planning to jump in, but Elmer tired of the chase and let him go before he got a ducking. His anger forgotten, the massive chimp agreed to go quietly back to captivity. This time the windows were made of double armour-plating and remained unbroken.

Chimps have strong individual characters and some are regular rogues. Another zoo had one, Compo, that had made a name for himself as a trouble maker. He could not bear to have the colony happy. With no provocation he would attack his fellows or his keeper, and the zoo decided that if he couldn't be moved elsewhere, he must be put down. Chester Zoo seemed to provide the answer, for Compo could be given his own island. He was large and moody and would spend hours glowering at the other animals as they played among the logs and trees on the islands. The keepers at Chester soon learned to treat him with reserve, for he had none of the affectionate habits of the others. The antipathy was mutual and the other chimps would not even look at Compo if they could help it. Because he was a disturbing influence he was taken from his island and confined in a large yard surrounded by a thirteen-foot-high wall. He seemed to settle down in his isolation for about a year, although he often alarmed visitors by thumping on the armour-plated glass let into the wall that separated him from them.

One hot day in June he succeeded in jumping to the top of the wall and escaping through a roof-ventilator which the gardeners had left open for coolness. It led him into the half-completed tropical house and from there he made his way to the public footpath surrounding the moat. Deliberately he demonstrated his freedom to the other chimps on their islands. It was too much for Solomon to stomach. Without further ado, he waded into the moat, crossed to the footpath and attacked Compo. There was a fierce struggle and when Compo realised he was no match for Solomon, he made off across the fields followed by two keepers. When he was some distance from the zoo, he turned to attack the keepers who were gaining on him. They were armed, and had no alternative but to shoot him dead. When they returned to the zoo at top speed to see what had happened to Solomon, they found that he had been quietly led to his quarters and all the others had been locked in their dens until they settled down again.

The problem now was that Solomon, having once crossed the water, might try it again. It was too big an operation to make the waterways wider and deeper and Mott decided to experiment with a low voltage electric wire similar to that used for confining cattle. Fortunately there was one in stock and it was immediately put round the islands, four feet from the edge and four or five inches above the level of the water. As soon as it was completed, the chimpanzees were liberated to see what would happen. The current was switched on and Mott stood ready to switch off if it caused too much distress.

Solomon was the first to move. He went straight to the point at which he had crossed and gingerly touched the wire. With a squeal he sprang in the air, wringing his hand in bewilderment. He looked at it closely, then reached out and once more touched the wire. Again he leapt in the air and chattered excitedly. Now he stood for several minutes, looking at the wire and appearing to make up his mind. The other chimps had not moved from their huddle, nor had they made any noise as they watched Solomon's performance. He shuffled over to them and, without making any sound or any discernible gesture, he walked up to each chimp in turn, looked into its face, then moved on to the next one. As he moved on, the chimp at whom he had last looked hurried over to the spot where Solomon had been shocked, and there they all stood in a semi-circle, their eyes fixed on the length of wire that he had touched.

Elmer now detached himself from the others, looked slowly round his fellows, and leaned out to touch the wire. He jumped back at the shock, paused to recover, then went in search of a willow twig on the far side of the island. Thus armed, he came back to the other chimps and leaned over to touch the wire with the twig. He screeched loudly at the increased shock conducted by the wet twig, and dropped it hurriedly. All the while the colony of chimps had watched motionless, but now they scattered and never went near the wire again.

This doesn't mean that they did not get into mischief in other ways. Solomon became a crack shot with sods of earth, and if anyone among the crowd took his fancy, he would heave a sod at them, scoring a bull's eye every time. When he ran out of ammunition, he would jump and gesticulate to his fellows on nearby islands. They got his message and would throw him a supply of sods which he would catch, pile into a small arsenal by his feet, and continue to rain on the public. His recognition was so acute that he could pick out any of the Mottershead family no matter how great a crowd surrounded the islands. It was invariably a signal to throw clumps of earth, various fruit peelings and debris by way of greeting. His disappointment when the offerings were not returned was pathetic, but Mott did not want to encourage the visitors to throw things at the chimps, and he had to set an example. But when he goes about the zoo in winter and there are few people about, he is not above joining the chimps in a bit of fun, and returning the sods that herald his approach.

On their island the chimps became different creatures from those kept in cages. Their fur grew thick and healthy and eventually they began to breed.

CHAPTER EIGHT

ANIMAL ANTICS

To anyone who studies animal behaviour, it is obvious that, within the framework of the species, each member is widely different from another. This is particularly apparent among monkeys and apes whose mannerisms and habits so closely follow those of humans.

In the realm of motherhood there could not have been two more different apes than Meg and Babu. Babu was watched closely by a keeper when it was noticed that she was pregnant, and she rewarded his interest in a manner that surprised him. He found her pressed up against the door leading to the passage when he came on duty one morning, and when he went to greet her, she held out her great fist and presented him with a new-born baby. It was only inches long, pink and scrawny and astonishingly like a premature human infant. As soon as she had handed it over, Babu bounded away from the door and could not be persuaded to take any further interest in it.

Rearing a chimp is almost identical to rearing a human. Both have to be nursed, bottle fed, winded, washed and coddled for many months. Fortunately the keeper had a wife and she took the baby into her home and raised it until it was big enough to look after itself and return to the colony.

When Meg showed signs of pregnancy a few months later, everyone quailed at the prospect of another five

1a – One of Chester Zoo's many baby giraffes.

1b – Mukisi, a mountain gorilla, deep in thought.

1c – A rare zoo baby, a rhinoceros with its mother

2a – One of Chester's bears enjoying an icy dip.

2b – Always curious, a sea-lion comes to get a closer look at the camera.

2c – Myra, the hippo, with her two-day-old son Bimbo.

3a – Pelicans in their paddock.

3b – Elmer, the chimp, trying to coax a duck towards him.

3c – A rare Spectacled Owl from South America.

4a – An American zoologist tape-recording the otters' 'speech'!

4b – The snapdragons proved too tempting for one elephant.

or six months' hard labour. But she proved to be a wonderful mother. Right from the first moment she gave her baby her whole attention, grooming it daily and carrying it everywhere she went, first in her arms and then, as it grew older, on her ankle which it sat astride. When it was a few months old and beginning to rebel against so much cosseting, it ran away from her, missed its footing and fell into the moat. Screaming in horror, Meg plunged in after it, scooped it up and in her anxiety, came ashore on the mainland where a large crowd of visitors had gathered. She enveloped her baby in her arms and crouched on the path chattering shrilly for help. When the keeper came, Meg flung herself at him, hiding her face in his jacket and all but asking to be taken back to the island.

Over the years Meg gave birth to ten babies, and as there must be a limit to the number kept at Chester, many of them were sent to zoos all over the world in exchange for other animals. When Meg had a baby in 1966, she was determined not to be parted from it. It had been thought that she had finished breeding and the arrival of Sally Ann surprised everyone. Mother and daughter were a joy to watch. The baby rode everywhere astride its mother's ankle as she gambolled round the island, appearing to have been rejuvenated by the birth. When feeding time came, the baby was not allowed to help itself. Meg pushed aside its hands and she herself chose which titbits to poke into the tiny mouth.

As the baby grew older and big enough to fend for itself, instinct warned Meg that the keeper might take it away. Newspaper photographers had often pictured her carrying her other babies, but she would not allow this one to be photographed. Visitors had only to produce a camera and Meg flew into a fury, stamping her feet, shaking her fist, and finally running to hide in the underground passage leading from the island to the inner dens.

It became obvious to the keepers that the baby was not developing as fast as it should. It took no exercise apart from clinging to its mother's leg, and it made no effort to feed itself. Plans were made to drug the food so that Meg would be sufficiently doped for a keeper to remove the baby, but before they could be carried out, Sally Ann died. Unable to realise the truth, Meg still tried to push food into the little mouth, and she persisted in carrying the body round with her, looking at it every now and again with a puzzled frown. The keeper drugged her food and removed the infant, and for a few days Meg was inconsolable, wringing her hands and searching every inch of her quarters for the missing baby. Soon the memory faded and she began to take an interest in her companions once more.

But the memory of Sally Ann must have remained, for when Meg gave birth to a son a year later, she rejected him completely. Never again was she prepared to love—and lose—her child. Meg was now aged twenty and a fully competent midwife. As soon as the baby was born, she pushed it through the bars of her den and chattered loudly until the keeper arrived, then she turned her back and went to sleep. The three-pound baby was handed to Mrs Dorothy Timmis, wife of the Curator, who had reared her own two sons as well as numerous lion and tiger cubs when she and her husband had lived in Taronga Park Zoo, Sydney. Every four hours, night and day, Tammy had to be bottle-fed until he was strong enough to sleep through the night. The problem was not keeping the chimp happy, for with the two Timmis children he had plenty of petting and company. But right from the start, Mrs Timmis had been told that as soon as he was old enough, Tammy must return to the zoo and take his place among his own kind.

Depriving an infant—human or otherwise—of the affection it demands is not easy, especially for a mother, and Mrs Timmis had to harden her heart when Tammy screeched from his play-pen, begging to be cuddled. The first time he saw his reflection in the polished wood of the drop-leaf dining table, he grimaced with fear, and when the time came for him to be returned to the zoo, he was allowed to take his little woolly jacket with him so as not to separate him wholly from his past. Another baby chimp was brought to keep him company, and after the first few days of sulking, Tammy accepted his new home and companion. The transition had been made in time, before he had completely identified himself with humans.

Solomon came to terms with his environment although he never lost his taste for adventure. Year after year he tried to entice the ducks and waterfowl using the moat to come ashore on his island. He learnt to move the water with his fist so that floating bits of food would be drawn towards him, and he never understood why it didn't bring the birds as well. His insatiable curiosity led him into disaster when a young keeper forgot to lock a door in the ape house. Solomon was a regular Houdini where doors were concerned, and only keys defeated him. When he found he could open the door, he bounded out looking for fun. All might have been well if a keeper had been on the spot. Instead Solomon walked right into a crowd of jolly schoolboys who scared the wits out of him. Panic-stricken, he made off over the fields towards open country and by the time the alarm was raised, Solomon was out of sight. He was spotted a little while later ambling along a road a mile or so from the zoo. Even then he might have been saved had he not been startled by a passing car. He bolted up a tree, straining his neck looking for a friendly face or a landmark. Then he saw a higher perch alongside the tree, a pylon carying overhead electric wires.

Forgetting his fear of wires, or perhaps not associating those with the ones round his island, Solomon reached out and grabbed the wire. There was a dazzling flash and the great chimp fell to the ground dead, just as a keeper arrived. He had spent eighteen years at Chester Zoo and he was mourned by thousands of regular visitors who had seen him grow and develop into a personality.

Although Mott welcomed the interest visitors took in particular animals, often coming long distances just to follow the progress of one creature, he was not happy with the system that allowed and even encouraged people to feed the animals. It was the practice in almost every zoo and he often wondered if he could stop it without offending the visitors who only meant to be kind. When he visited Frankfurt Zoo in 1953, he was surprised to find that it was an offence to feed the animals. He asked the director if there had been any protest from the public when the rule was instituted and when he was told 'no', he made up his mind to prohibit feeding in Chester Zoo.

Notices were put up asking visitors not to feed animals and, surprisingly, only three people complained, one of whom was a regular visitor who had not the remotest idea of what animals should eat. On one occasion she had brought a bucketful of sour green plums which she had fed to a polar bear. It was desperately ill for two days and in great pain. Other creatures had not escaped so lightly. A very tame hornbill died after someone gave it a mothball, and another bird was killed by a cough-drop. Apart from such dangers, there were perhaps twenty or thirty thousand people visiting the zoo on some days and even moderate offerings were enough to blunt the animals' appetites for their balanced diets.

From the time the new rule came into effect, the health records of the animals showed a marked improvement, and although the food costs went up—now it all had to be bought—the animals received fair shares and their minor illnesses could be diagnosed immediately instead of being put down to over-eating titbits.

Unfortunately ostriches are gluttons and, like babies, seem to enjoy putting foreign bodies in their mouths. Ozzie had been off colour for two or three days and when Mott was showing round an Army officer, he remarked that he would not be surprised if Ozzie had swallowed the padlock from his door. The keeper had lost one and Mott put two and two together and did not like the result.

Viewing the problem from a military standpoint, the officer said, 'Why don't we go over the ostrich with a mine detector? It will let us know if there is any metal inside the bird.'

A team of soldiers complete with mine detector, the vet and Mott, watched by a crowd of press photographers, gathered in Ozzie's pen for the experiment. The bird was held captive while the instrument was placed near to his feathers and moved slowly over his body. There was no doubt about it, the detector showed that Ozzie was harbouring metal in his stomach.

When everyone had gone, the vet anaesthetized Ozzie and there in his stomach was the missing padlock. He recovered from the operation for a day of two, and then relapsed and died. A post mortem operation showed what the mine detector had missed; a second padlock stuck in his gizzard. But Ozzie did not die in vain. A new type of lock was fitted to the doors, one that could not possibly be eaten, even by an ostrich.

Although he knew every one of his animals individually, Mott could not always anticipate their actions. He was having a great deal of trouble with the telephone one summer, and as the zoo was becoming a complex organisation with incoming calls from all over Europe, a considerable amount of extra work was caused by the frequent breakdown in communications. A conversation might start satisfactorily, but halfway through the connection would be cut off. Complaints were made to the GPO and telephone engineers overhauled the switchboard at the zoo in an effort to trace the trouble. But still it continued, bedevilling everyone.

One day it reached a head. Mott was in the middle of an important conversation when the lines became jumbled. He put down his phone and went to look for someone who could call from an outside line to complain again. By force of habit he glanced at the animals he walked by, in particular at George, a magnificent giraffe that seemed to be uncommonly busy concentrating on something. Usually George was very friendly and came over to greet anyone who passed by. Mott paused, then looked again. George had stretched to his full eighteen feet, leaning his head over the top of his wire enclosure, and was busy licking the telephone wire that ran parallel to his fence. Mott immediately sent a message asking the telephone engineers to come at once. They confirmed his suspicions; George was the culprit and his licking had been causing all the chaos. They suggested elevating the telegraph poles several feet to take the wires out of reach of the giraffe.

While the gang of men worked, George followed every movement, walking backwards and forwards on the other side of his fence keeping in step with the workmen. He leaned over to sniff at them on their ladders, and watched with interest when the wire was lifted on to the new high poles. Only when the men had finished their work and were packing their tools did he spring into action. He stretched as far as he could and then more, poked out his eighteen-inch blue tongue, wrapped it round the telephone wire and pulled. The whole day's work was wasted, and the wire had to be attached to even higher poles.

George's exploits made amusing reading in the newspapers and he became a celebrity. People came just to see him and the attention went to his head. He was quite happy when visitors stood outside his fence admiring him, but let them turn away as if to leave, and he stretched his neck over the fence and tried to grab their hats. Frequently he succeeded and visitors had to be warned to stand well back. It was all harmless fun and George was invariably gentle when he snatched at hats and caps, but apart from the inconvenience of having a keeper permanently on guard to rescue headgear, there was the danger of George swallowing wire that might have been used in hat trimming, and once again the fence had to be raised to end his game.

Even so George had the last word. It had been thought by everyone at the zoo that giraffes were mute, but on the day that George found he could no longer make contact with his visitors he roared, proving that they can give voice when sufficiently excited.

Jimmy, an orang-utan, was four years old when he arrived at the zoo and puzzled everyone by his habit of walking upright. He spent his first few days exploring the orang island and waving, boxer-style, with his hands clasped over his head, to the visitors. Once he was familiar with the other orang-utans, he lost interest in the island and casually waded through the moat to the mainland where he mingled with the crowds and went for walks round the zoo.

No matter how often keepers caught up with him and

enticed him home, he invariably waded ashore as soon as the coast was clear. Mott decided to put a single-strand electric fence round the moat, similar to the one round the chimp island. But Jimmy suspected a trick and strode over the wire without making contact. Another stand was added, making the fence too high to be straddled, and for a few days Jimmy paced the perimeter, deep in thought. His solution was to uproot the wooden support, bringing the whole fence down. A more complicated fence was installed on much stouter posts, but it did not obstruct him for long. He learnt, by trial and error, to short-circuit the fence by draping a length of weed from the wire into the water.

Keepers were instructed to keep a constant watch on Jimmy, but as time went on he tired of strolling round the public paths with people, and became interested in his companions on the island. But his curiosity may kill him yet. A careless visitor threw a plastic bag into the moat and Jimmy fished it out and ate it. For days he hovered between life and death and only prompt medical attention saved him.

Belinda, the six-foot high bear, son of One-Lung, was not so lucky. When he was thirteen, someone dropped the plastic top of a vacuum flask into his enclosure. It tasted sweet and the trusting bear swallowed it. It lodged in his stomach and, despite an emergency operation, Belinda died.

The most popular bird in the zoo was Gorgeous, a roseate cockatoo that had been presented in 1952. He had been a pet and he loved to perform for visitors, dancing and whistling and bending his head to be scratched. At the the beginning of 1965 a keeper on his evening rounds found that the door of the aviary had been forced, and Gorgeous was missing. The police were informed, but there was little hope of finding him.

Two weeks later, however, a pet shop in Liverpool reported having bought a cockatoo that resembled the one missing. A keeper was sent and promptly identified Gorgeous. For the journey back, he was put in a cardboard box, but he soon chewed his way out and travelled the rest of the way whistling and dancing on his perch on the back seat of the car. Subsequent enquiries showed that the thief was a self-styled bird lover who admitted having stolen a number of smaller birds from the zoo over a period of years. Now he had been discovered, he asked if he could have a job working with birds. Mr Mottershead put his foot down firmly. He had learnt to beware of people who, while waxing sentimental over animals, were irresponsible sometimes to the point of cruelty. As proof that liberation had not been a kindness, Gorgeous never really recovered from his kidnapping, and died the following year.

Most monkeys are individualists and incurably mischievous. Tookie, a Mona monkey, insisted on washing every morsel of food before eating it. Charlie, another, was an expert pick-pocket and keepers had to empty all their pockets before entering his cage. He and his mate, Minnie, had been presented to the zoo by Mrs Netta Robinson who had reared them from babyhood in her home in Kwale, Western Nigeria. The babies had been brought to her by African hunters who had shot the mothers for food.

Minnie and Charlie were more dead than alive when they arrived, but careful nursing transformed them into healthy animals. Charlie had begun stealing right from the start, and stored the objects in his cheek pouches. Often when Mrs Robinson called him to his meal, he would slap both his cheeks and disgorge a mouthful of coins, lead shot and even lipsticks, which he had been hiding. Fortunately he was intelligent enough not to swallow any. When the monkeys grew older and became vicious, they were no longer suitable as house pets and were sent to Chester Zoo where they engaged in a friendly war of wits with their keepers, stealing hose pipes and chewing holes in them, and once flooding out their cages.

CHAPTER NINE

ELEPHANTS UNSHACKLED

As Molly got older, Mr Mottershead looked round for another elephant, both as a companion to her and to replace her in the event of her dying. In 1949 he was asked if he would accept Barbar, an obstreperous Asiatic female from Whipsnade Zoo. She was a fully grown twenty-year-old, surprising everyone by settling down immediately she arrived at Chester and not living up to her reputation. She was gentle with Molly, as if understanding she was in pain, and mourned pathetically when, a few months later, Molly died.

A dealer from whom Mott had ordered a rhino cabled to say that, while he could not supply one at present, he had a pair of baby elephants. They turned out to be five-year-old African males, just the sort of challenge that Mott had learnt to take in his stride. African bull elephants are known to be the hardest animals to keep captive. They reach a weight of three tons when fully grown, eleven feet in height, and are able to destroy virtually anything that man can erect. But when they arrived, Rascal and Bobo were only half grown and were put in the empty rhino house.

Rascal had a violent temper and could not be trusted out of sight. An elephant is both intelligent and cunning; if it takes a dislike to anyone it will bide its time until that person drops his guard. The elephant will then move with remarkable speed and try to crush its enemy against a wall. Fortunately, Rascal and Bobo liked their keeper and the worst mischief they did was to steal from visitors. They disliked the 'no feeding' rule and when they saw children sucking ice cream, they would stretch out their trunks and try to grab the cones. Cigarettes, gloves, coats and cameras were wrested from unsuspecting visitors, and one day when a priest escorting a Sunday School party round put his satchel containing a dozen prayer books on the wall, Rascal seized it. Before the startled priest could find a keeper, the elephant had eaten his way through the lot, leather case and all, fortunately with no ill effects.

Bobo's greed taught him cunning. He took his place at the head of the nightly queue for a loaf of bread, stuffed it quickly into his mouth and doubled back down the line to the back of the queue, hopeful that the keeper might overlook the first loaf and give him a second. He never lost hope, although his ruse was never successful.

As the two elephants grew, they set about wrecking their home. Destruction comes naturally to them, for in their native land they think nothing of pushing down a tree just to reach the tasty leaves at the top. Like captive elephants the world over, they were chained each night to prevent them pushing over the walls. In spite of being restricted, they stretched their trunks and poked holes in the roof, and it was obvious that it was only a matter of time before they demolished the building.

For years Mott had been studying his elephants and designing the ideal enclosure that would give the animals maximum freedom while not exposing the keepers to danger. Rascal and Bobo were the only two African bull elephants in Britain, and by the time they were fully grown, it was essential that they should be housed so that they would not be a menace to all around. In addition, Mott disliked having to shackle them with chains: it was against all his beliefs and he was determined to find other ways of confining them. But no one could advise him. Other zoos either kept their elephants in chains or refused to have bulls at all. It was an accepted fact that no one could make an elephant do anything it didn't want to. Rascal and Bobo were such loyal companions that chaining them in separate stalls seemed unkind.

Anticipating problems such as this, soon after the war ended Mott had asked the authorities if he could have the anti-tank road blocks that were scattered round Cheshire. Surprised that anyone should actually want them, the authorities told him he could have as many as he needed on condition he paid for their removal. A local contractor gave an estimate for delivering all the anti-tank blocks within a ten-mile radius, and in due course a thousand arrived, along with an assortment of pill-boxes and concrete slabs. They became the basis of the finest elephant house in the world. The animals were separated from the public by a low wall and a wide ditch. They were able to come and go at will, and there were two large pools, one inside and one out, where they could bathe whenever they wished, day or night. Their outdoor paddock covered an acre and adjoined the hippo enclosure. Inside, tropical plants climbed up the roof-supporting pillars and tumbled in profusion. The large island area was divided into sections, any one of which could be isolated by barring the entrances with metal rods built into the walls. This could be done without a keeper having to enter the enclosure.

The elephants settled down at once and soon began to thrive as they never had before. With frequent mud baths, their skins became smooth and supple, and exercise in the huge paddock improved their condition immeasurably.

Two Asiatic female elephants were the next to arrive.

A dealer asked if the zoo could accommodate them temporarily and Sally and Judy, both aged five, moved in. Within a short while the zoo bought them and a year later bought Sheila, a fifteen-year-old African elephant. The moment she walked into the paddock, Bobo detached himself from the others and claimed Sheila as his own. Like a lovesick teenager he followed her every movement, brought her choice bits of food, and spent hours twining his trunk around hers. The others accepted the love affair with good grace, particularly Rascal, who had been Bobo's inseparable companion.

Mott began to hope that his great ambition, to be the first zoo in the world to breed an African elephant, might be realised. He had a sufficient number of elephants to stimulate natural feelings of rivalry, and the animals had too much to interest them in their surroundings to become bored. As well as the numerous visitors who were now coming to Chester all the year round, a pair of hippopotami, Jimmy and Myra, moved into the Pachyderm House with the elephants. Their enclosure was separated from the elephants by a five-foot wall, and the ground level of the hippo paddock was several feet lower than that of the elephants.

When the hippos appeared for the first time, the elephants gathered along the top of the wall and bellowed a greeting. Jimmy and Myra took no notice of them, but went for a swim in their own large pond. In their outdoor paddock, again adjacent to the elephants, they found that the sunniest place was against the party wall. Rascal took the opportunity of prodding them with his trunk, and when this had no effect, began to blow down Jimmy's ear. The hippos were immensely tolerant, and contented themselves with snorting when they had had enough. The elephants never tired of studying their neighbours, but always in the friendliest possible way.

In March 1964 Mott had good reason to believe that Sheila was pregnant. She and Bobo were still devoted to each other and were recognised by the rest of the herd as inseparable. On Wednesday the eighteenth the keeper rang Mott to express his concern about Sheila's appearance. Her head had begun to droop and she showed signs of exhaustion. Mott hurried over, took one look and decided to send for the vet. He went to make the telephone call and on his return found the elephant lying on her side, dead.

Bobo was pacing backwards and forwards beside her, trumpeting his alarm, and all the other elephants were in a cluster shuffling their feet. Gradually they were enticed to their outdoor paddock and the door closed to keep them out while the vet made his examination. All the recognised tests were made but no sign of disease or accident could be found. It could only be assumed that she had died of heart failure, not unknown among elephants. She was too big, at nearly three tons, to be moved, and Mott had to make the heartbreaking decision of having her butchered. Economics had to come before sentiment, and of her £1,000 value, at least some could be salvaged by using her flesh as food for the other animals.

Manageable pieces of elephant meat were put into the huge refrigerator to be stored. The paddock was scrubbed clean and the other elephants allowed to come in. Everyone thought that was the end of the matter, as well as the end of Mott's dream of breeding a baby elephant. Sheila was the only mature African female in the herd.

Meanwhile, a keeper of small mammals decided to give his animals a treat. He took a hunk of the elephant meat from the refrigerator and fed it to his racoons, pine martens and an American badger. Twenty-four hours later they had all died, and he was honest enough to confess his action. Tests showed unmistakable traces of anthrax, a disease as old as history that kills both man and beast. Ministry of Agriculture officials were called in and although further samples of the elephant meat seemed harmless, later they developed typical anthrax cultures.

The elephant enclosure and small mammal house were cordoned off and quarantined, and massive doses of penicillin were given to every living creature, humans included, in the zoo. The elephants looked distinctly distressed and still missed Sheila, but Mott hoped that they had been treated in time.

The following morning, Sunday the 22nd, he went into the elephant house as soon as he got up, not waiting to have breakfast. He will never forget what he saw. Bobo lying dead in the pool and Rascal on the side. Barbar was inconsolable and paced round the bodies, gently touching them with her trunk, while the only other live animals, Sally and Judy, huddled together looking fearfully round them.

There was no question this time of carving up the bodies to facilitate removal. The danger of spreading the infection was too great. Somehow they had to be got out whole and destroyed completely by fire. Once again, the living animals, now only three, had to be shut outside, despite the cold winds, while workmen pulled down part of the back wall, built a ramp across the moat, and brought in tractors and winches to haul out the great carcasses. Police supervised the entire manoeuvre, and specialists brought flame guns and huge oil burners to consume the bodies.

For two days and three nights the pyre burned, and Mott mourned his loss. The three surviving elephants were given daily doses of penicillin, and the surfaces of the paddock, both indoors and out, were gone over with a flame gun to burn away any traces of infection. In addition, several inches of topsoil outside were removed and replaced with fresh clean soil.

Then, a week later, Sally the baby Asiatic elephant collapsed and died. An autopsy showed that although she had had anthrax, she had actually recovered from it and had been killed by too much penicillin. Only Judy and Barbar remained, and they wandered endlessly round their quarters, desolate for their companions.

Still the bad luck that had dogged the elephants had not run out. Soon after the anthrax outbreak, a dealer who had heard of the disaster offered to send four young elephants. Spirits rose but were again dashed. The four youngsters had been so badly handled and neglected that when they arrived at Chester they all had to be destroyed.

In Rhodesia Lieutenant-Colonel and Mrs R. A. Critchley of the Wild Life Conservation Society of Northern Rhodesia were caring for a baby bull elephant that had been found abandoned in the Luangwa Valley. He had spent a year with them on their ranch near Lusaka and although he was completely tame, he was rapidly outgrowing his home. Now he was to be presented to Chester Zoo.

Jumbolino, aged two and weighing half a ton, was flown into London in August, his crate loaded on to a truck and taken to Chester. He arrived at the zoo at two o'clock in the morning and was given a rapturous welcome by Judy and Barbar whose mother-instincts had been severely curtailed by the death of their companions. Now they fussed and petted the new baby as though he were a toy. Jumbolino had not seen another elephant since he had been abandoned at the age of six months, but he recognised his own breed and brought new life to the elephant house.

He made friends with the hippos and startled his

keeper when Jimmy opened his mouth and Jumbolino put his trunk right into it. It became a favourite game, the trunk sometimes being replaced by a foot, and the hippo never closed his mouth until the elephant had removed himself.

Sheba was the next Asiatic elephant to arrive and she was immediately adopted by Barbar. All four got on very well but like most elephants, they had a wicked sense of humour. When Judy began balancing on the wall surrounding the moat, showing how she could 'tightrope' walk along the narrow ledge, Barbar crept up behind and gave her a push. She bellowed with rage when she lost her balance and fell eight foot into the ditch, and roared even louder when she found she could not get out. The keepers came running, saw that only her pride was hurt, and led her round the ditch to the gate leading to the paddock. After that she waited until Barbar was playing on the wall, when she charged and got her own back. A similar tumble ended in tragedy at London Zoo when Diksie was killed after being pushed into the ditch.

No sooner had the four at Chester learned to live as a family, when a dealer telephoned Mott and asked if he could help him. He had a young Asiatic bull elephant, Nobby, ordered by another zoo which, upon inspection, was found to be unsuitable. Being a responsible dealer, he would not allow his animal to go to a bad home, and was now saddled with it. Would Chester Zoo accept it as a boarder?

Nobby was separated from the other four in a small section of the Pachyderm House fenced off with two iron bars. But not for long. The lonely little animal trumpeted his distress then flattened himself on the ground, spread-eagling his legs to lessen his height, and crawled beneath the bars to join the group. Judy promptly abandoned Jumbolino and went to mother the newcomer who was so much smaller and more timid.

Jumbolino resented the newcomer and did his best to get rid of him. If Judy was not looking, he would charge Nobby, almost knocking him over. Barbar and Judy combined to protect the baby. They sandwiched him between them and pushed Jumbolino away when he tried to squeeze in and butt the interloper with his miniature tusks. When these tactics failed, he went on a hunger strike and although Judy seemed upset at his sulks, she would not abandon Nobby.

Keepers had been following the situation closely to see that it did not get out of hand, when one morning Jumbolino lay down in the paddock and refused to get up. There was an uproar. Perhaps remembering the tragedy of their former companions, Barbar and Judy strode round their enclosure, their trunks aloft, trumpeting in alarm. Other animals in nearby enclosures took up the cry until it seemed that every inmate was calling for help. The elephant keeper knew his charges and diagnosed a mammoth dose of jealousy. He fussed over Jumbolino, persuaded him to get to his feet and eat a bag of buns and titbits, then slipped away, leaving him to the others.

Judy and Barbar rushed over and stood closely at either side to prevent him falling. They explored every inch of his head and neck with their trunks, and when they had satisfied themselves that he was all right, took charge of him.

Jumbolino remained slightly jealous of Nobby until he discovered him as a companion with whom he could play squirting mud. After that they became firm friends, sometimes ganging up against their elders and having to be disciplined with slaps from Barbar's trunk.

In 1966 the zoo in Basle, Switzerland, announced the birth of an African elephant, the first ever in captivity. It was born some months after the date Sheila and Bobo would have had theirs, the gestation period being twenty-two months. They sent a photograph of the baby to Mott, and although he had little hope of living long enough to achieve his ambition of breeding an elephant in Chester, he was delighted that another zoo had succeeded.

CHAPTER TEN

MOTTY IS BORN

Some of the rarest animals in the world are the square-lipped white rhinos which are found in only two small areas: the Sudan, where they are in danger of becoming extinct, and the Umfolozi Game Reserve in Zululand. Umfolozi is the home of the square-lipped rhino and from an estimated herd of twenty in 1847 there are now over six hundred.

Early in 1962 the Natal Parks Board in South Africa offered a few of these rhinos to accredited zoos throughout the world. Chester Zoo was included. Mott replied immediately; at £3,000 each they were among the most expensive animals alive, but Chester asked for a pair. June and her husband, Fred Williams, were sent out to Africa to see the animals in their natural habitat, study their needs and accompany them on the long sea journey home.

This was the first time that the rhinos had ever been exported, and the job of finding a safe and suitable means of capturing them was given to Mr Ian Player, Senior Game Ranger at the Umfolozi Reserve. With the use of a drug developed by Dr Harthoorn of Kabete, Nairobi, Mr Player and his rangers developed a technique which enabled them to capture a fully grown rhino and transport it hundreds of miles without upsetting it.

As soon as June and Fred arrived at the Reserve, they

were told that a hunt was taking place next day and were invited to go along and watch. First thing in the morning the Zulu game guards were sent to locate the herd, especially the animals required, a large female ordered by the Kruger National Park, and a small female for San Diego Zoo in California.

June and Fred were taken by Land-Rover to a rendezvous with the game guards who reported that they had located three rhinos, a large male weighing about three and a half tons, a female a little smaller, and a little female calf weighing about a ton and a half. The guards described the type of country where the herd was grazing, for everything depended on the Land-Rover being able to follow the animals until it was within twelve to fifteen yards of them, this being the effective range of the 'Cap-Chur' gun.

It was decided that the two females would be suitable and drugged darts were prepared, the amount of tranquillizer being adjusted to the weight of the animals. The large female would be travelling about five hundred miles and it would be better if she were drugged for the whole journey so that she would awaken in her new home.

As soon as everything was ready, they set off following a trail of broken branches marked out by the game guards. Mr Player stood on the back of the Land-Rover with his dart gun and as soon as he sighted the rhinos, he signalled that the hunt was on. The rhinos picked up their heels and ran unbelievably fast when they caught sight of the vehicle. Overhanging branches scraped along the Land-Rover's sides and small bushes were flattened. When they were within twelve yards of the rhinos, the gun was fired and a dart struck the rear of the smallest animal.

Two horsemen now took over. They did not attempt to chase the animals, but merely kept them in sight.

Soon the rhinos stopped running and began to graze, and within fifteen minutes the one that had been drugged lay down. One of the horsemen stayed while the other returned to the Land-Rover to guide it back. He explained that the male and female had not left their calf.

Mr Player kept his gun ready with the second dart and off they set. The male and female began to run when they saw the vehicle, but the female did not run far. She wanted to protect her calf and although she bolted in alarm when the dart hit her, she quickly slowed down and finally collapsed only a short distance away.

Meanwhile a crate had been brought and placed in front of the calf, a small amount of antidote was injected into the animal causing it to stagger to its feet just long enough to be steered into the crate, and it fell asleep again. The door was fastened and the crate winched on to the back of a five-ton truck.

The horsemen chased off the male and now began crating the large female. Very little antidote was given to her and although she managed to stand up, she seemed unable to walk. All hands were needed to shove her into the crate where her legs buckled beneath her and she was out cold. She was loaded on to the second truck and taken to the Kruger National Park where she settled down immediately.

Chester's two rhinos were caught in a similar way but the male, Madagiwe, was shot with a dart intended for his mother and therefore had a stronger dose of tranquillizer than would normally have been given. When he was brought back to the holding pens, the Zulu game guards opened the crate expecting to see him bound out and race round the enclosure. Instead he was still half-doped, and he staggered out, reeling from side to side. The guards began laughing and shouted 'Madagiwe' which, in Zulu, means 'drunken one'.

Madagiwe and his mate Madageni became quite tame during the long journey home. In preparation for their arrival a new rhino house was built in the record time of three weeks, during which stonemasons and staff worked non-stop. The house, made of sandstone and roofed with transparent plastic, was one hundred feet long by fifty feet wide, with a large outdoor paddock. Inside the heated building were planted masses of hydrangeas and fuchsias. A wall was built to separate the white rhinos from the resident black pair, Susan and Roger. They all made friends and rubbed noses in a neighbourly way, but that was the extent of their fraternisation. Trouble would soon have ensued had they been allowed to invade each other's territory.

The veteran polar bear Punch and his companion Judy grew old together, and the improvement in their health, caused by their having a swimming pool, prolonged their lives. When Punch died, it was estimated that he was forty-one years old, a great age for a polar bear, captive or free. Judy was obviously lonely without him and began to take more notice of visitors, standing on her hind legs and stretching out her neck to get a better view. Unfortunately she gave the impression that she was begging and all manner of unlikely objects were thrown to her. Potato crisps, ice cream cones and orange peel may not have done her any good, but they probably did not do her too much harm. But less responsible people didn't stop at that: they threw rubber balls, plastics wrappings and even metal toys. As a result Judy became seriously ill and a keeper had to be posted by her enclosure to prevent visitors from poisoning her further.

Meanwhile Mott began building a new, larger polar bear enclosure covering half an acre with a pool big enough to accommodate a whole family of polar bears.

Remembering that the zoo owed so much to Punch and his protector, Mott erected a plaque on the wall which read, 'To the memory of Miss Catherine Jane Tompkyns-Grafton of Fellborough, Windermere, as a token of gratitude for her interest in the polar bears and for her generous legacy which has enabled the Society to make so many improvements for the well-being of the animals and birds at Chester Zoo.'

Soon afterwards the zoo received the pair of polar bears it had ordered from a Continental zoo. Judy was never introduced to them. It was decided not to upset her by moving her to the new enclosure. Like so many animals, she knew she was going to die and was happier in her own familiar surroundings where she could be undisturbed.

Rack and Ruin were nearly three years old when they arrived and soon Mott realised they would never breed: they were both females. He started looking for a male bear and eventually was able to get one in exchange for a pair of lions. Chester was becoming famous for its strong healthy lions which were exported to zoos all over the world.

Rubble, a male a little younger than Rack and Ruin, was welcomed warmly by the others. As the bears grew to maturity they were very different from their predecessors, bigger and stronger and with far more spirit. When their pool froze over one hard winter, they hurled themselves on to it on their stomachs, like animated rugs on a polished floor, but when they began testing its surface as a spring board from which to leap to freedom, the keeper drained the pool, causing the ice to cave in, and once again the enclosure was escape-proof.

In preparation for the day when they might breed, one of the inner dens was equipped with under-floor electric heating. In the wild, the pregnant female bear holes up in a small snow den which is heated from her body, but in captivity infant bears die if artificial heat is not provided. When Rack approached the time for her confinement, she was enticed into the warm den and isolated from the others, as she would have been had she been living in the wild. Extra food and vitamins were given to her and she was left entirely undisturbed. On December 3rd 1959 she gave birth to a cub. The keepers usually name offspring of their charges, and the polar bear was called 'Motty' after Mr Mottershead. Motty was a female and she thrived. When she was about three months old and her mother was getting tired of being locked in her den, the other two had to be taken to their dens so that mother and child could get some exercise.

Motty enjoyed waddling around the pool and chasing her mother's shadow, but she would not go near the water. Time after time Rack plunged in, swam round and came to the water's edge to coax the little one in, but Motty backed away and snarled if her mother tried to force her. One day she was playing with a raw herring, in the way that a kitten plays with a ball of wool, when it fell on the slope leading to the water. Motty gambolled after it, got into a skid and fell with a splash in the pool. Her mother swam over from the opposite end but Motty had recovered from her initial shock and could not be persuaded to climb out. Later she grew the thick fur on the soles of her feet that helps polar bears in the wild to keep their grip on ice.

The other bears hated being locked up, and they hurled themselves against the gate trying to break loose. Usually they were only locked up for the very brief occasions twice a year when workmen repaired the great holes that the bears made in the concrete. Even then they did their best to break out, and it was a nerve-racking experience for the men to have several tons of enraged bear only a few feet away. After a time the bears became so cunning that they refused the bait offered to entice them into their dens and sometimes it took the keepers three days to succeed in penning them.

When Motty was six months old and strong enough to withstand a rough and tumble, Ruin and Rubble were released into the enclosure. Keepers stood by armed with high-pressure hose pipes in case Motty was attacked, as cubs frequently are by their fathers, but Rubble obviously did not recognise his daughter as such, and accepted her without incident. The long period of transferring bears from the enclosure to the dens to give the two sets their fair share of exercise was a big price to pay for a baby bear. Mott was glad to have bred Motty, if only to prove that it could be done successfully in his zoo, but he did not intend to make it a regular occurrence in case the close confinement affected the health of the bears.

Giving animals conditions as near as possible to those to which they have been born is often a real worry. When Mott acquired the only pair of mountain gorillas to come to Britain, he went to some lengths to study their needs. Mukisi and Noelle were about three years old and had been captured in the Congo where the government exercised strict control to prevent them becoming extinct. In their natural state, gorillas live in family groups and care for their young with such fanatical devotion that it is usually necessary to kill a whole group of several families to capture one baby. Their chief requirements in captivity are warmth and humidity indoors and plenty of room for exercise outdoors.

Over the years parts of the dream tropical house were being built jig-saw fashion. First to be erected was the section housing the chimpanzees, followed by the nocturnal house and now, on the west side, work began on the huge structure for the gorillas. An island was built outside to provide a place where they could play, surrounded by a moat, and a tunnel connected it to an inner enclosure.

Until their new quarters were completed, Mukisi and Noelle stayed in the chimpanzee house, and before long they began to lose condition. Their skin became dry and they persisted in pulling patches of hair out of their coats. It was only a localised complaint—their general health was excellent—but it was a symptom that all was not well.

Work was speeded up on their new home and within days of their being installed the gorillas showed a marked improvement. They stopped pulling out their hair and began to grow thicker coats. In addition their physique improved and the dryness of their skin disappeared. The warm moist air inside seemed to harden them to the cold outside, for even in the coldest weather, when the snow lay thick, the gorillas spent most of the day out of doors, just coming in to get warm before going out to play again.

The most expensive animals in the zoo, Mukisi and Noelle were valued at £3,500 each. Soon they were joined by a pair of lowland gorillas, Gogal, a female aged three and weighing forty pounds, and Boko, a male, aged eighteen months and weighing twenty pounds. They were very tame and clung round the keeper's neck whenever he went near them, begging to be cuddled and taken for a walk. To help them settle down, he spent an hour each day playing with them until gradually they gained enough confidence to play on their own without having their hands held by a human.

Like all monkeys and apes, gorillas hate to be laughed at and, even more, they hate to see humans pulling faces at them. Students of animal behaviour have reason to believe that contorted faces denote threats of aggression in the animal world. Certainly such expressions either terrify them or send them into a violent rage, often upsetting them for days. Without doubt it is an act of cruelty, and notices were erected outside the enclosures asking the public not to tease the animals.

On the other hand, gorillas are full of fun and like nothing better than to have an appreciative audience when they play. If there are no humans around, they perform for their neighbours the orang-utans which occupy the next island and have adjacent indoor enclosures. Gorillas, although so much stronger than orangs, are not so destructive. Heavy rubber swing doors had been fitted on to the tunnel leading to the island. The gorillas played with their door, swinging it backwards and forwards and trying to clout each other with it, jumping with glee when they succeeded. But after a few days they tired of this game and let the door alone. The orangs, however, first dismantled their door and then painstakingly reduced it to confetti. More seriously, they started to eat it and were very sick until the vet dosed them to clean out their systems. A stronger rubber door was installed, reinforced with nylon, and this defeated them. Annoyed, they took a dislike to it and delighted in kicking it each time they went past, becoming even more cross when it rewarded them with a smack on the rump if they didn't get out of the way in time.

CHAPTER ELEVEN

BIRDS FLY FREE

The post-war boom in zoos was world-wide and the International Union of Directors of Zoological Gardens, which Mr Mottershead had joined in 1950, grew from strength to strength. In 1962 he was elected their President for a three-year term, and he and his wife went to the annual conference held that year in San Diego, California, at the beginning of their first world tour of zoos.

In San Diego Zoo—rated as one of the best in the world—he saw koala bears exhibited for the first time. They are one of the few animals that cannot be kept in Britain because they cannot live without the eucalyptus trees which provide their food.

From America Mr and Mrs Mottershead flew to New Zealand where, as well as seeing the two zoos, they were reunited with their elder daughter, Muriel, who had married and emigrated almost ten years before. Mott spent some time in Auckland Zoo where, in spite of a delightful setting and absolute cleanliness, he disliked the prison effect caused by so many iron bars. The Superintendent, Mr Derek Wood, was an old friend who had worked in Chester Zoo before taking up this appointment.

After New Zealand they went to Australia where, at the Taronga Park Zoo in Sydney, a former keeper Bill Timmis was in charge of several gorillas. Bill was to return to Chester later and become the curator of mammals.

From Australia Mott went to Japan where a new zoo was being built, incorporating many of the best features that had evolved in other zoos.

The conference the following year was to be held at Chester, and on his return Mott set about speeding up the building of his tropical house which, he now knew, was unique. Nothing he had seen even approached it and he hoped it would be in full operation by September 1963.

The greenhouses were stocked with a large variety of tropical plants, many of which had been grown from seed sent by friends of the zoo in all parts of the world. A wide variety of tropical birds had been ordered and it seemed as if the tropical house would be ready well in time. Then, in the middle of December 1962, a gale caused thousands of pounds' worth of damage in one night. Large sections of the roof blew off the almost completed tropical house and were wrecked as they were tossed willy-nilly about the grounds. The lions and tigers had been locked in their dens when the storm began, but a tree fell on the fence of the deer paddock and a Père David stag escaped. He returned to his paddock the next morning, but during his hours of liberty he had eaten poisonous shrubs and was very ill for a few days.

But the most severe result was the set-back in repairing the tropical house. Now it could not be ready in time for the conference. Delegates came from as far as Pretoria and Rome, Washington and Helsinki, Warsaw and Copenhagen and heard papers on subjects ranging from clouded leopards to the breeding of Humboldt's penguins. Wives of the delegates were entertained by the Duchess of Westminster and Lord and Lady Tollemache, and Lord Leverhulme proposed the toast at the dinner on the final evening. As he sat surveying his important guests from faraway places, Mott couldn't help smiling to himself at the change in the fortunes of his zoo. Such a short time ago he had been scrubbing out cages while his wife and daughters had earned a few badly needed shillings making teas for the visitors. Now he was receiving congratulations on all sides from people whose opinions mattered and who asked for his advice. He felt very proud.

When the conference ended, Mott went back to his tropical house. It was to be quite different from most zoo buildings in that visitors would be able to wander about freely in the tropical vegetation while birds of several species would be free to fly and nest anywhere. Fibreglass was being used as extensively as possible in walls and ceiling to allow the maximum sun and light to penetrate.

A problem that presented itself out of the blue was the great number of sparrows that moved in as soon as the roof was on. After considerable effort they were cleared out, only to come in again by way of the swing doors in the gorilla and orang tunnels. Zoo sparrows are unafraid of wild animals and soon learn to dodge them. Eventually they were kept out when the tunnels were reconstructed with a twist so that the birds could not see and were forced to fly in darkness. It stopped the mass invasion, but a few of the cheekier sparrows still flew in to get warm and have a good feed.

On the north side of the tropical house a new reptile section was built with large cages that faced into the house, and on the south side sleeping quarters for the chimps were erected.

In early spring, gardeners began planting the stock they had been growing for eight years or more, when the tropical house had been a mere mirage on Mott's horizon. Climbers were set against the pillars supporting the roof, ferns beside the alligator pool, orange, lemon and banana trees, along with hundreds of sweet scented shrubs, gardenias, lilies and exotic plants from as far afield as the Galapagos Islands.

It was decided to formally open the tropical house on June 13th 1964, the Society's 30th anniversary, and the animals, birds, crocodiles and alligators were moved in. For the first few days Mott hardly slept, the problems came so thick and fast. For a start, he had not envisaged the change that would come over the alligators and crocodiles. Normally lethargic and slow-moving, they came to life and not only snatched food from their keepers instead of waiting, immobile, for it to be thrown to them, but also lay in wait for any bird to come within snapping distance.

Birds that had been bred in captivity showed no instinct for survival. They had forgotten how to fend for themselves and were killed by predators or drowned in the fountains, seemingly unaware of danger. Several hummingbirds and an Indian Hill Mynah landed near the alligators and were instantly swallowed, and Desmond, a magnificent toucan with an eight-inch beak, was snatched from an overhanging branch at least two feet from the surface of the pool. The alligator responsible had leapt in the air to snatch his prey, to the astonishment of a visitor who reported it to the keeper.

Soon after the tropical house was opened, Mr and Mrs Mottershead set off on a second world tour of zoos which had asked him to address their zoological societies. From New York they went to Detroit and Chicago and in Dallas he was asked to give a talk, illustrated with colour slides taken at Chester Zoo. Then he was made an Honorary Citizen of Dallas.

In Canada they journeyed to the Columbia Ice Fields, 7,200 feet high, and saw wapiti, deer, moose and beaver in their natural setting. After touring several zoos in

Canada, they went to Fiji where fourteen inches of rain fell in one hour, and on to Australia where the annual conference was to be held in Taronga Park Zoo, Sydney. The Executive Director of the Taronga Zoological Park Trust, Sir Edward Hallstrom, spoke of the rare birds of paradise in New Guinea where there was a sanctuary, and Mr and Mrs Mottershead were invited to visit the island. They were flown deep into the interior and then escorted by natives to the forests where the trees were thick with birds of the most gorgeous colours. Many of the leaves had been stripped as if by a plague of locusts but, using sign language, natives explained that the culprits were birds of paradise that peeled the leaves into shreds.

Mott was determined to acquire some of these birds now that he had a tropical house with the right climatic conditions, and he began making enquiries about buying some, no easy matter when they were controlled in order to prevent their extinction. Each year they were increasingly decimated by natives who killed them for their vivid feathers required for ceremonial headdress.

After leaving New Guinea, they toured the South Island of New Zealand then travelled to Melbourne, Adelaide and Perth, studying animals and birds under varying conditions. Their journey took them to the Cocos Islands and Mauritius *en route* for South Africa and the Kruger National Park. But before reaching their destination, Mr and Mrs Mottershead had to equip themselves with tropical clothes and, accompanied by Dr Brand, Director of Pretoria Zoo, they set off up-country from Johannesburg for the Skukuza Camp where they spent several nights in native-style huts.

In the National Park, Mott spent several days fascinated by the large number of elephants, lions and giraffes as well as the great herds of impala, then on through Swaziland to Umfolozi, the home of the square-lipped white rhino. They broke their journey at the Imperial Hotel in Piet Retief, Natal, where the proprietor, hearing that his guests were zoo directors, invited them to see his pet. It was the biggest lion they had ever seen, weighing about a thousand pounds. Althought it was obviously a male, it had no sign of a mane, but had a head like a lioness. It was perfectly tame and docile and shared an enclosure with a Saint Bernard dog, with only a six-foot fence of wire netting to keep it in.

At Umfolozi Mr and Mrs Mottershead were invited to join a hunt to capture white rhinos, and Mott was pleased to see for himself the humane methods in which no animals were harmed or even frightened during their transfer from the Reserve to zoos.

Back home in England, Mott rushed to his tropical house as soon as he arrived in Chester. He was amazed at the change. Shrubs and trees had shot up during his four months' absence and although minor skirmishes had broken out among the birds, most had learnt to live in peace and keep out of each other's way.

A pair of kiskadees had proved the exception. Yellow and brown flycatchers from South America, they had seemed to settle down at first, but no sooner had the other birds built nests, than the kiskadees set to work destroying them and throwing out the eggs. The problem was how to catch them. In a huge house, exactly like a stretch of jungle, looking for a particular bird could prove a job for life. The head keeper remembered that the kiskadees often flew down the passage behind the reptile cages to steal from a bowl of small fish kept there for feeding. It was decided to use their greed as bait. A bowl of fish was put in the passage at the end of which was an empty reptile cage with the door wide open. As soon as the kiskadees arrived for their fish, a keeper went to the end of the passage and drove the birds into the empty cage. They were then transferred to a large aviary in the tropical house, reserved for trouble makers. Eventually they built their own nest and succeeded in rearing young.

Hummingbirds and sunbirds caused a great deal of trouble in the first few months, fighting and attacking any other bird that crossed their path, but as the vegetation grew and became more dense, limiting their vision, they chose their own territories and caused no further casualties. The first season, too, nearly all the birds joined in to attack the hibiscus plants, breaking off the flower buds just as they were about to blossom, but in subsequent years they lost interest and the plants were allowed to burst into a riot of colour.

The tropical house had been in operation almost a year when word came that a consignment of birds of paradise was on its way from New Guinea. The thirty-seven birds, costing £9,000, travelled to Sydney by boat where a member of the staff at Taronga Park Zoo met them and escorted them by plane to London. Ten different species were included in the consignment, some of the rarest and most beautiful birds in the world. The ribbontails had three-foot long tail feathers, the Carol six-plumed had three narrow feathers projecting from either side of its head—or it should have had; the one that was included in the batch arrived with only three, having broken off the other three during the journey. And perhaps the most beautiful specimen of all was the Prince Rudolph, otherwise known as the blue bird of paradise, with long fluffy tail feathers, magnificent blue colouring on his back and a deep green head.

A large free-flight aviary had been prepared for them in the tropical house, but Mott wondered if they would prefer to live at large with the other birds, nesting at will in the now luxuriant vegetation. Certainly they would make a splendid spectacle flying like huge jewels among the multi-coloured foliage. He decided to experiment by releasing just one, the Prince Rudolph whose progress he could watch. He had not long to wait. The bird made a quick tour of the house until it found the banana tree. It settled on a topmost leaf and began tearing it to shreds, throwing down the bits like so much confetti. Mott tried to make it stop. He flapped his arms about and called out to the bird, but it took no notice. It stripped the great fleshy leaf right down to its centre vein, then it hung, upside down, displaying its beautiful plumage for all the other birds to admire.

If Mott had hoped that it would settle for one plucked leaf, he was going to be disappointed, for a moment later the Prince Rudolph set about tearing another leaf to bits and then another. The tree was beginning to look as moth-eaten as those in the jungles of New Guinea by the time the bird was recaptured and safely locked inside the aviary where bamboos had been planted, but definitely no banana trees to tempt him to further destruction.

Feeding the two or three hundred birds that inhabit the tropical house proved to be much more simple than had been anticipated. Each species chose a territory and nested there, returning at bed and feeding times. Keepers filled numerous dishes with different fruits, grain, wheat germ and insects and the birds soon selected the diet they preferred. Bottles filled with nectar were fastened to trees and refilled several times a day, and became a great attraction for the visitors who had only to stand quietly near such a tree and within a short while tiny tropical birds came to feed. The tropical house attracts many more visitors in winter. Although it is humid, it is entirely suitable for humans and it has become a haven to which they can retreat from the fogs, snows and the cold.

The birds of paradise, still the biggest collection in Britain, were given a special diet consisting of mealworms and mice as well as locusts—their natural food in New Guinea—specially bred in Chester Zoo for them. They had been used to eating pawpaws but they quickly accepted bananas and soft pears, varied with a mash of codliver oil and hard-boiled eggs, and before long they began building nests, a sure sign that they had accepted their new home.

CHAPTER TWELVE

PROBLEMS WITH PATIENTS

With an ever-increasing population of such varied inhabitants, the zoo employed a full-time vet to take care of the animals' health, and a hospital was built in which patients could be isolated. Mott had always been a firm believer in giving nature a chance, and he refused to interfere when animals gave birth unless complications were expected. His instincts proved sound; other zoos' experiences had taught him that when giraffes, for example, are helped into the world, the babies are frequently deformed.

Monkeys and chimpanzees, while quite able to deliver their babies themselves, often refuse to rear them and they would die if immediate attention were not forthcoming. Jeannie was born to Meg one windy autumn day but instead of weighing between three and four pounds, the normal birth weight of Meg's other young, she weighed only one and a half pounds. After making a close inspection of the skinny infant, Meg handed it to a keeper and refused to have anything more to do with it. By the time it was brought into the hospital it was very cold and almost dead. Its breathing stopped and immediately it was given the kiss of life. Jeannie clung desperately to the tiny thread of life. She was given glucose and milk every hour, night and day, until she was strong enough to suck from a baby's feeding bottle. Then she suddenly began to thrive and gain weight.

Six weeks after Jeannie's birth, Babu gave birth to Polly and promptly abandoned the baby. Polly was a fat healthy youngster and she was brought along to the hospital to be reared with Jeannie. Girl-keepers took them over and mothered them, taught them how to drink from a cup and gave them the companionship they needed. When they reached the age of three they were transferred to the apehouse to be introduced to other small chimps with whom, eventually, they would share an island.

New arrivals were sometimes put in the hospital if they had had a long journey that might have disturbed them. Now that Chester Zoo was world famous for its excellent conditions, it was often asked to take creatures which might be proving an embarrassment to the authorities, so when the Customs and Excise officials confiscated two rare Siamese gibbons from a man who was trying to smuggle them into Britain, they were offered to Chester Zoo. Mott was delighted to take them. Because of their decreasing numbers in Sumatra, their native land, they are on the list of protected animals and are very rarely seen in captivity.

These two, a male and a female, had bad colds when they arrived and had started to go bald on the crowns of their heads. They were put into hospital and given extra vitamins and very soon they began to look better and stop pulling their hair out. Obviously they had been upset by their travels and were needing the security of a permanent home. Three weeks after their arrival they were transferred to an indoor monkey house where they could become acclimatized before going to live out of doors.

It was quite another story when Dora the chimp became ill with flu. The keeper brought her to the hospital and she was admitted to a warm cage and given medicine and extra vitamins. But instead of getting better, she grew steadily worse. Mott went to see her and she clung to him like a baby, whimpering and burying her face in his neck. He offered her food but she knocked it out of his hand, and when he tried to detach her from his jacket, she screeched and shook her head, working herself into such a rage that a keeper had to be called while Mott made his escape. He came again the next day and Dora was in a pitiful state. She sat crouched in a heap on the floor, her eyes bleak with misery. Although the vet could find no reason for her regression, there was no doubt that she was getting worse. Mott decided to take a chance. He picked her up and carried her out of the cage.

'Come on, old girl,' he told the drooping chimp. 'You're going back home.'

A keeper was told to bring a spare cage and install it inside Dora's sleeping den where she could be kept warm and given regular food and medicine and remain undisturbed by the other animals. She went into it without persuasion and began to accept whatever was given to her, taking a keen interest in all that went on although she obviously had no desire to join in the play of the other chimps. Within a few days she had completely recovered and rattled the cage bars, begging to be let out.

Mott had learnt another lesson. The cure can be worse than the complaint, and whenever animals could be treated *in situ*, they were to be left among their own kind. He realised that an animal as sensitive as Dora might have fretted herself to death if she had not been returned to her own quarters in time.

Sometimes sick animals help each other to get better. When Winifred, a giant anteater, came to the zoo she was only six months old and so feeble that it was expected she would not survive. Nevertheless she was put into the hospital where she went into a corner, turned her back on the world and refused to budge. In the next cage was a palm civet, a tiny furry creature like a puppy, called Joe. He had cut his paw badly and had been put in hospital so that it could be kept clean and dressed daily. He took an immediate interest in his new neighbour and, as he was allowed out of his cage during the day, he went visiting. They became great friends, snuggling up together and communicating with odd snuffles and grunts, and within a few days they became so distressed when the keeper came to part them at night, that they were allowed to stay together. Long after Joe's paw had healed, he stayed in hospital to keep Winifred company, and when they were both discharged they were given a stall in the camel house where they could live together. Winifred grew to a great size, but even when she dwarfed her little friend she was always gentle with him and utterly devoted.

From time to time birds from outside are brought in with oil on their wings and are admitted and treated. A razorbill found on the Isle of Anglesey, where he had crawled exhausted out of the sea, was brought in by a returning holidaymaker. The bird had to be bathed with detergent and water and then caged until his feathers acquired enough natural oil to enable him to fly. Fortunately he had not tried to get clean himself, or he would most certainly have poisoned himself with the oil. He became quite tame during his stay at the hospital and when he was released he stayed in the grounds for several days before deciding to return to the wild.

Although there is an operating room fully equipped to cope with any emergency, many operations are carried out in the animal enclosures, with excellent results. When Turvy the Malayan bear attracted the keeper's notice by the way in which he kept hugging his face and holding his head on one side, the vet was called in. He could see that the bear's face was swollen on one side, which indicated a dental abscess. Turvy was enticed into a small 'crush' cage in which he could not turn round or thresh his limbs about, and injected with one of the modern wonder drugs, Phencyclidine, which put him to sleep within ten minutes. He was then pulled out of the cage so that the vet could remove the offending tooth. When Turvy came to some time later, he was back in his own den none the worse. The drug had been discussed at the Zoo Conference held at Chester when several directors confirmed that it was the best and safest tranquillizer they had tried. It was capable of anaesthetizing an elephant. Many drugs, while safe in themselves, can kill animals if the exact dose is exceeded, but the safety range of Phencyclidine was such that up to four times the required dose would still not kill the animal.

A more difficult operation was performed on George, a large alligator, for the removal of a growth in his mouth. He showed signs of having difficulty eating and the vet drugged him so that he could be hauled out of his pool and examined. It was a simple matter cutting out the growth, but the keeper was told to bathe the wound with antiseptic each day if possible, and without tranquillizers or anaesthetic. As first George was reluctant to open his mouth, and the keeper equally reluctant to try forcing him. But after a few tussles, the alligator seemed to realise that the treatment was easing his pain and he became a model patient. After he had been better several months, he climbed out of his pool and insisted on opening his mouth when he spotted the keeper. Obligingly, the keeper bent down and looked in, to discover that the alligator must have been in considerable pain with an abscess on a front tooth. Once again he was given daily treatment and he made a full recovery as well as establishing an unusual rapport with his keeper.

One winter a surprise patient arrived in the arms of a sailor. It was a young snowy owl that had landed on board the M.V. *Sir Andrew Duncan* which was on its way to Birkenhead. During the journey the bird had dined royally on dressed chicken from the ship's deep freeze and it was in excellent condition on reaching port. As soon as it arrived at Chester Zoo it went on hunger strike and was admitted to the hospital where it was forcibly fed. When he was sure that there was nothing physically wrong with it, Mott took it into an aviary where a resident pair of snowy owls lived. He stood by in case of a fight, but the pair fluttered round it flapping their wings and scuffling. The newcomer remained still, its wings half-opened but making no move to defend itself. Then the pair calmed down, hopped on to a long perch and moved up to make room for the new arrival. There were no more feeding problems; the snowy owl settled down immediately.

Many animals suffer from the same troubles that beset humans. Maud, the fifteen-foot giraffe from Somaliland, was prone to gumboils, especially when she was pregnant, and if they were not treated promptly, she would lose her appetite along with her usual good temper. Keepers try to keep on good terms with giraffes for they can inflict serious damage not only with kicks, but with swipes from their necks which they use as weapons. When Maud went off her food and began rocking her head from side to side, the keeper brought his ladder, leaned it against the fence and persuaded the giraffe to come close. One look in her mouth was enough to show the trouble, and the vet prescribed hot water mouthwashes plus antibiotic injections. The pain made her obstreperous and sometimes she refused to open her mouth despite the coaxing and pleading of the keeper as he struggled on the top of his ladder holding the bucket of warm mouthwash. Often he had to climb down and replace it as it cooled and the contrary giraffe, as soon as she saw him leaving, would rush to the fence and lean over, opening her mouth for him.

Albert and Henry, two cheetahs who came to Chester eighteen years ago, began to suffer from toothache when they reached their mid-teens and needed dental treatment. Now they are practically toothless and must have all their meat minced for them. Sometimes they snarl at their legs when they feel twinges of rheumatism, but regular sunray treatment and an occasional aspirin keep them healthy. In their wild state they would have died years ago when their teeth started to decay and made them unable to catch and kill deer and other prey. In the zoo they have a large paddock fenced with chain-link where they can dream of the days of their youth when they could run at seventy miles an hour. One of their few 'wild' characteristics that remains after a life-time in captivity is their insistence on only freshly killed meat, preferably rabbit and chickens. Cheetahs seldom, if ever, take carrion or re-visit a kill, and Albert and Henry are no exceptions.

A pair of Malayan tapirs, Scotch and Soda, proved to be faddists when they arrived at the zoo. Although they were only a few months old, they were as large and as strong as grown pigs, but not so dependable. Scotch bowled over the keeper when he was cleaning out the enclosure, and set off at top speed for the open country. The alarm was sounded and a posse of keepers took up the chase, finally catching up with Scotch four miles away where he had taken refuge in an evil-smelling pool. A keeper managed to get a rope round the tapir's neck and was preparing to haul him out when the animal jerked his head, propelling the keeper into the pool with him. Both had to be hosed down on their return to the zoo.

In their natural state tapirs eat, among other things, branches of trees and Mott always tries to keep as near as possible to animals' native food. But Scotch and Soda turned up their long noses at all the branches offered them. Other foods were introduced and the animals' re-actions studied. They rejected vegetables but liked milk and then, quite by chance, they tasted the branch of an apple tree—and demanded it daily.

During the winter they became ill with stomach trouble and despite treatment with antibiotics, showed little improvement. Again Mott tried them on various foods in the belief that animals will eat what is good for them, given the opportunity. Scotch and Soda were interested in nothing until they had their first taste of yoghourt. It was the turning point in their illness and they drank pints of it every day until they were well again. Then they had to be weaned off it and back to their natural food.

One of the more serious operations was performed on a clouded leopard, Jason, the first ever to arrive in Chester. He was eighteen months old and nearly five feet long, with teeth like those of a sabre-toothed tiger. On his journey to Britain with his mate, Mimi, Jason injured a front leg. Although he was treated on arrival, infection had set in and the leg had to be amputated.

The animal recovered well from the operation but Mimi went into a decline fretting for her mate. Mott and the vet considered whether to equip Jason with an artificial leg, but they decided against it. There would be too much danger of its getting stuck in crevices of trees in the enclosure, and experience had shown that animals losing a limb soon learn to manage well without it, strengthening their other limbs in compensation. But Jason could not be put back with Mimi until he was stronger and until the stump had completely healed and hardened. The dilemma was solved by a young keeper, John Sumner, who appointed himself sparring partner for the frustrated Mimi. Each day in between chores, John entered the enclosure and romped with the leopard, bracing himself to catch her as she leapt at him, ripping strips from his overalls. Although one of the most vicious and unreliable of the cat family, the clouded leopard tempered her strength to her keeper, baring her fangs but not digging them in, showing her claws but not using them.

By the time Jason was well enough to take over, Mimi had become thoroughly tame and at first missed her bouts with the keeper. Nature asserted itself, however, and John did not make the mistake of trading on past friendship. He had filled a temporary need and his reward had been transient promotion to the world of animals. Now he was just another human who was advised to keep well away from his charges.

No two creatures are alike and although every inmate has a dossier listing its habits, date of birth or arrival, country of origin, history of health and peculiarities of temperament, Mott and the vet often have to adjust the treatment to fit the individual. Many animals do not mind having a limb in plaster when it is broken, so long as they are isolated in a smaller cage where they can rest undisturbed for the few days it takes for them to recover. But when the Griffon vulture broke his leg, he made a terrible fuss as soon as the plaster cast was put on. It was quite a small cast and not very heavy, but the bird refused to stand and lay on the ground, his wings outspread as if he were dying.

Mott offered him tempting titbits but the bird wouldn't be soothed. He screeched at the top of his voice although he was in no pain. Mott told the vet to remove the plaster at once. The vulture quietened while it was being cut off, then fluffed out his feathers and got to his feet, tucking the injured leg beneath his wing. He was transferred to a smaller cage where he could reach his food and water dishes without having to move, and a week later his leg bones had knitted together and he was plucking the bars of his cage with his strong beak demanding to be returned to his own enclosure. Once again an inmate had prescribed his own treatment.

Even when animals die, the zoo's interest in them does not end. Mott works in close co-operation with several universities and when he has a dead creature, he telephones round to see if any department is doing research which might benefit by examining or dissecting a part of the animal. Thus one university will ask for the brain, another for the stomach and a third for a paw. Detailed reports of their findings are sent to Mott and are sometimes of use in the treatment of living animals. When one report said that the animal concerned had had a calcium deficiency, others of the same species in the zoo were immediately given additives to their diet.

Visitors sometimes ask if they can buy the skins of dead animals for rugs, but they are always refused. Animals that have died either from natural causes or following accidents, such as swallowing foreign bodies, leave skins that would be useless for any form of decoration. The hair or fur comes out in tufts and can seldom be properly cured. And, above all, Moss is violently against the wholesale slaughter of wild creatures by hunters who want the heads and skins as trophies. He longs for the day when people will regard such mementoes not as status symbols, but as proof of the hunter's selfishness and cruelty.

CHAPTER THIRTEEN

PETS NEVER FORGET

Every week letters come to Mott asking his advice on how to choose pet monkeys and chimps and how to train them. In every case he begs would-be owners to think again before trying to domesticate such animals, for although they start off as delightful companions, most develop bad habits and even viciousness when they reach maturity. Then they are usually sent to a zoo where they feel themselves abandoned.

One of the first pet monkeys to be brought to Chester Zoo was one that had belonged to a doctor who had been taken ill and could no longer care for it. It had been treated like a baby, even to sharing its owner's bed, and, in fact, regarded itself as a human. As soon as Mott put it into a cage it flew at the wire in fury, screaming its head off demanding to be let out. It refused to eat or drink, but spent all day with its face pressed up against the wire in an effort to look up the path. Each time it heard approaching footsteps it began to get excited and do handstands and cartwheels. And each time its expected owner failed to materialise, it sank back into apathy. At the end of the week its eyes had dulled and it no longer looked for the loved one. It had given up hope. Mott telephoned the doctor and told him that unless the monkey was taken home at once, it would fret itself to death. But the doctor could not take it back, and he had the heartbreak of asking

Mott to painlessly destroy it.

Pooh, a South American capuchin monkey, was fifteen years old when he came to Chester and he had been a house pet all his life. Capuchins are about the best-tempered, most affectionate monkeys of all, but even they sometimes prove too much for their owners, demanding as they do the sort of attention needed by a very young child. But children grow up, while monkeys behave like infants all their lives. Pooh was fortunate in that the zoo already had two capuchins which welcomed him as a friend. But he never got over his need of humans. The keepers did their best to provide the necessary contact but their time was limited and Pooh frequently had to be forcibly detached when playtime was over and they had to get back to work. He is over thirty years old now, but he has never given up hoping that one day his master will come for him. When visitors stop by his enclosure, he sits on his best behaviour looking anxiously for the never-forgotten face. And when his disappointment is too hard to bear, he clutches his chest and whimpers pathetically, feigning an illness that will bring him extra attention from the keeper.

When Viscount Spencer Alexander Churchill went to spend some time script-writing in America, he brought his three-year-old chimpanzee, Ernie, to Chester Zoo. It was a hard decision for him to make, but Ernie was such a one-man pet that it was inadvisable to leave him with the Viscount's staff at his Mayfair flat.

The chimp brought with him his own pint pot, a toothbrush and a cigarette holder through which he smoked. Master and pet shared a last cigarette at the zoo before they parted and Ernie was introduced to the other chimps. At first he refused to leave his sleeping quarters and would have nothing to do with his companions. All day he sat hunched in one corner, fingering his three treasured possessions and sobbing quietly to himself. He would only come out of his gloom when the keeper picked him up and gave him a cigarette, when, for a few minutes, his eyes would brighten and become alert. But as soon as he realised that he was not being taken home, he would lapse once more into his misery.

His companions, Kim, Mary and Susie did not know what to make of the sulky stranger and Susie began to tease him, trying to steal his toothbrush or his cigarette holder. Fearing trouble, for even the gentlest of chimps can become extremely ferocious if their temper is aroused, Mott had Susie moved to another group. Once she had gone, Mary, the friendliest of animals, began to mother the newcomer. Each time he whimpered she scurried over to him and put her arms about him, rubbing her cheek against his, and before long they became inseparable. But she never approved of his smoking, and when the keeper brought his weekly cigarette, Mary would take herself to a far corner and sit there wrinkling her nose in disgust.

Viscount Churchill wrote regularly asking about Ernie's welfare, and although the chimp settled down eventually, he still looks wistfully at the crowds, perhaps trying to remember what his master looks like.

Jason was a three-year-old fifty-pound lowland gorilla that had been brought up in a small private zoo in Spain. Mott thought he would be the ideal mate for the resident female gorilla, Gogal, but when they were introduced, Jason screamed in terror and would have nothing to do with the bewildered Gogal. It appeared that Jason had not seen a gorilla since babyhood when he left his mother, and as he now identified himself with humans, he was terrified when faced with such a strange animal. Left on his own he began to fret in the familiar pattern, but unlike many former pets, he seemed willing to transfer his affections to any human instead of pining for just one. Mott instructed the keepers to let him out of his cage whenever they had the time spare to take him for walks round the zoo to give him confidence. It worked like a charm. Several times a day the little gorilla walked hand in hand with a keeper, pausing to chatter to the giraffes or the lions, and occasionally springing into the keeper's arms when startled. Each walk began and ended by Gogal's enclosure and soon the two gorillas were on speaking terms. Jason still refused to eat unless the keeper sat beside him in the cage, but he spent more time looking out to see what was happening and less in fits of depression. Eventually the two gorillas were put together for a few minutes' play and little by little Jason learnt to live with Gogal without fear. Everyone breathed a sigh of relief for Jason was rapidly gaining weight and strength and soon it would have become unsafe to allow him to walk at large.

Circus animals that are handed to the zoo present no problem. Life in Chester must seem like heaven to them after a life on the road, and when Prince, a performing chimpanzee, arrived, he spent his first few days turning cartwheels, while the rest of the colony stared in amazement, then tried to copy him, while he rocked with laughter as they failed. He loved it when crowds gathered, and he would put on an impressive one-chimp show, beginning with a war dance accompanied by realistic war cries and ending by hurling a clod of earth into the centre of his audience. If they failed to applaud, he would encourage them by clapping his own hands. Several years after his arrival, Mr Mottershead's three-year-old granddaughter, Joy, pedalled her tricycle near to the chimpanzee island and Prince made such a fuss that the keeper came to investigate. Words were not required to explain the excitement; during his circus days

Prince had performed on a uni-cycle and had never forgotten. Now little Joy was bringing back memories which he wanted to share.

A chimp with a mysterious history was Ufiti, or 'evil one'. Although she was a native of Gambia, she had turned up in Northern Nyasaland and it was believed that she had escaped from captivity, for she seemed lonely and deliberately sought human company. Being the only chimpanzee at liberty in the whole of Nyasaland, she became quite a tourist attraction and people would motor for miles into the bush just to see her. At first she was happy to take offerings of fruit from them, rewarding them with a handshake, but after a time she turned savage and actually attacked some of her benefactors. She was captured and the Governor of Nyasaland, Sir Glyn Jones, who had visited Chester Zoo, thought it would be the ideal home for Ufiti.

She was flown to London and brought the rest of the way in a heated van, and keepers were warned to take no chances with her—animals that have savaged humans rarely reform. But Ufiti surprised everyone. From the moment of her arrival she was the perfect resident, eating whatever was given to her and kissing the hands of the keeper who fed her. Whatever had turned her against the people in Nyasaland was now forgotten. Ufiti had buried the hatchet. It was winter when she arrived and she was quartered by herself in an inside cage. At first she took no interest in the other animals, concerning herself solely with visitors and keepers, but gradually she began to be curious about nearby residents. In the spring she was taken to chimp island and a keeper stood by on guard, prepared to rescue her if necessary. She seemed surprised at first to find so many replicas of herself, but at least she knew she was one of them, and after a few minor skirmishes to demonstrate who was the boss of the colony, Ufiti was admitted without further trouble.

Animals other than chimps and monkeys that have been house pets do not fret to the same extent, but they always seem to need some human affection. An Indian mongoose, Peter, went wild when first put into a cage in the Mammal House, tearing round the sides and flinging himself against the door. Fearing he would injure himself, the keeper let him out, giving him the freedom of the house. Peter got over his display of temper and took to following the keeper on his rounds, walking just a few inches behind him. At night he slept in the keeper's locker and made himself invaluable by keeping down the mice that frequented the building. Occasionally he slipped through the door out into the zoo grounds, but always came back before the keeper went off duty, and when the regular keeper was transferred to another section, the mongoose immediately attached itself to the new man, although he always remembered his first friend and would run towards him and climb up his leg if they met.

Animals' long memories never failed to astonish Mott. When a party of officials from the Congo came to see for themselves how the rare mountain gorillas had settled down, they were taken on a tour of the zoo. As they entered the tropical house and approached the island on which the gorillas have their indoor enclosure, the animals began to behave strangely. They lifted their heads and yelled, clenched their fists and beat the air and gave every sign of throwing a fit. While the officials watched their antics with interest, murmuring to themselves as to the cause, Mott began to feel uneasy. He kept a wary eyes as the gorillas searched the floor for anything that might serve as a missile. He was not mistaken. Finding nothing inside, the male gorilla hurried to his outdoor enclosure and returned with a huge lump of concrete in his hand. Without pausing in his stride, he flung it at the head of one of the Congolese. Mott anticipated the attack and managed to push his guest out of the path of the missile. The concrete weighed over five pounds and might easily have killed the man had it found its mark. Shaken, the men were hurried out of the tropical house, while Mott explained that the gorillas had never tried to attack anyone before. He could only assume that from early infancy, gorillas in their wild state are taught to recognise the appearance of those who threaten their existence, in their case, coloured humans, and to attack before they themselves are attacked.

In a similar way chimpanzees become agitated and nervous when coloured people visit them. Although coloured people are employed in the zoo, they are never put in charge of the apes. An odd sidelight on animal behaviour is the fact that it is not only the animals that were captured in infancy that show fear of coloured people. Even those that have been born in Chester Zoo demonstrate the same fear, possibly prompted by racial memory, the little known phenomenon by which memories are passed down from generation to generation.

CHAPTER FOURTEEN

ESCAPES AND ALARMS

As the zoo prospered and attracted more visitors, its finances rose correspondingly and, following the terms of the Society's charter, were ploughed back to improve the amenities. As adjacent land came on the market it was bought, until the original nine acres had grown into three hundred. Mott's waterway system was extended and, fed by water from an artesian well, it was almost two miles long. Regular water-buses were run so that visitors could travel from exhibit to exhibit, breaking their journey to see the animals without having to walk great distances. There are eleven miles of footpaths in the zoo and not everyone has the energy to walk them all.

The waterways are linked to the moats surrounding the animal islands, but these are not navigable. On one large island, built primarily for waterfowl, Mott tried keeping a colony of gibbons. The man-made island had been too bare to accommodate anything at first, but when the poplars, willows and rhododendrons matured, it seemed an ideal home for them.

The first pair was installed and a small wooden house built for them among the bushes. They were a great attraction as they leapt from tree to tree, covering more than twenty feet in one leap. Another pair was put with them and for a time all went well. Keepers went over each day by boat taking food and cleaning out their den, and when the water-bus sailed by, the whole colony gathered at the water's edge to wave and hoot to the passengers. Later, when the two females had babies, the little ones clung to their mothers' waists like living belts, not seeming to mind when the gibbons swung from branch to branch with breath-taking speed.

The first hint that all was not well came on a warm summer's day when the zoo was doing a roaring trade and there were water-bus trips every few minutes. A man who had once looked after the gibbons before they were moved to the island was put on relief duty on one of the water-buses. The gibbons did not like him and obviously bore him a grudge. Whenever they saw him passing by on the mainland they were in the habit of screaming curses at him and shaking their fists. Now, when they caught sight of him in the boat, so much nearer to them, it was too much for one male. He launched himself from the topmost branch of a tree, flew through the air and landed on the cabin roof of the boat. One or two children who were passengers screamed in alarm, but the gibbon took no notice of them. He jumped on to the hated keeper with bared teeth and savagely attacked him. Fighting the monkey off with one hand and shouting for help, the keeper made for the mainland where other keepers, who had heard the cries, were waiting to help.

The gibbon was overpowered and taken to a cage, but not before it had inflicted considerable damage to the keeper's arm, tearing away his clothes and clawing and biting the flesh. The water-bus was immediately re-routed so that it no longer sailed round the gibbon island, and once again the animals lived in peace. But not for long. When the water froze during a cold spell, the gibbons had high jinks sliding across the ice to the mainland and rushing back to the safety of their home when anyone approached. But one gibbon, bolder than the rest, came ashore and began exploring the zoo. He was caught before he managed to do any mischief and put in a cage on the mainland until the thaw set in. When he was taken back to the island two or three weeks later, the others would not accept him. They flew at him as soon as he stepped out of the boat, and the keeper had to come to his rescue and return him to the mainland. His repatriation was attempted again but with the same result. He had been outlawed by his tribe and could never live with them again.

Another stretch of water encircles the penguins' island but it is blocked so that the birds cannot swim away from their own section. When two Humboldt's penguins were hatched, there was great interest to see how zoo-bred youngsters would differ in their habits from those bred free. In the wild, Humboldt's penguins build their nests some distance from the sea. When the chicks are hatched they are fed by their parents on regurgitated fish until they are about four months old. By then the chicks are as big as—and considerably fatter than—their parents who suddenly realise they have done their duty. They promptly take themselves off to sea for a well-earned rest. In a short time hunger drives the young penguins out of the nest and instinct guides them to the sea where they soon learn to fend for themselves.

Robert and William reacted exactly the same as if they had been hatched wild. Their parents stopped feeding them, and when the chicks found that their plaintive cries had no effect, they both set off in search of the sea. They escaped from their escape-proof moat and were spotted swimming round gibbon island. Keepers tried to net them from boats, but by nightfall the penguins had found their way to another section of the waterway, this time behind the giraffe house.

For two days there was no more news and Mott was

afraid they had been killed by foxes which frequent the neighbourhood and carry on eternal guerrilla warfare with the smaller birds and animals. Then a police message came from Ellesmere Port, six miles away, where a penguin had been seen on the Manchester Ship Canal. To reach the nearest point of the Canal it had travelled on foot over a mile of fields separated by thick hedges. A keeper hurried to Ellesmere Port, but once again the penguin evaded capture.

Meanwhile Robert reappeared in the penguin moat, now quite prepared to acccept food from the keeper and settle down. The next day William was seen in the middle of Chester in the canal by Tower Wharf, approximately nine miles from where he had been seen at Ellesmere Port. He ventured into a lock where an RSPCA inspector caught him and returned him to the zoo. Having obeyed the call of the wild, he never wandered away again.

The same could not be said for Ferdinand the Third, a bison with a taste for adventure. A century ago there were sixty million bison roaming the prairies of America and although Indians killed them for meat and hide for clothing, it had little effect on their numbers. When the West was opened up by settlers, millions of bison were indiscriminately slaughtered, their hooves made into glue, their tongues canned and their flesh used to feed the railroad builders. And buffalo hunting became a popular sport, encouraged by ranchers who begrudged them the grass they grazed. By the turn of the century, the bison had almost been exterminated and the few that remained were rigidly protected, national parks being created in which they could live unmolested. Gradually the herd increased and bison were sent to zoos all over the world to ensure that they would not become extinct. Such an animal was Ferdinand the Third.

Like his predecessors at Chester Zoo, he laughed at the efforts made to confine him to his enclosure. Times had changed since the first bison had tickled his tongue with electric shocks. Now the paddock was surrounded by a low wall and a wide ditch, but they presented no problem to Ferdinand. One night when the keepers had gone off duty, he took a flying leap and cleared both obstacles. He had enough sense not to keep to the main paths where he might have been spotted by Mr and Mrs Mottershead during their evening stroll. Instead he set off across country and was miles away by morning.

A cowman sent to gather his herd of pedigree Ayrshire cows just as dawn was breaking rubbed his eyes in amazement when he saw Ferdinand, twice as large as life in the meadow with them. The bison looked enormous next to the cows, and he pawed the ground in the manner of a bull about to charge. The cowman raced back to the farm to tell his employer and fetch help. The farmer telephoned the zoo; Mott went to the paddock and found Ferdinand missing, and the farmer and his cowman went back to the field to keep an eye on the cows and await the arrival of the keepers who were bringing a truck to remove the intruder.

But Ferdinand was quite happy where he was, surrounded by coquettish cows who were obviously welcoming his attentions. So much so, in fact, that he could only be enticed aboard the truck if Buttercup went first. And Buttercup seemed so overcome at being pulled away from the bison that the farmer took out his diary and made a few pertinent notes of dates. He forthwith notified the zoo that if his pedigree cow gave birth to a hump-backed calf, he would have to sue them for damages. Mott was not alarmed; the zoo has to be insured against such risks. On the other hand, the farmer stood to make a tidy profit if such a cross-breed calf were born alive, possibly the first ever to be born in Britain.

It was an anxious time, not helped by Ferdinand who kept breaching his wall and ditch and going in search of Buttercup and having to be tracked up and down the neighbourhood. But the Ayrshire cow was delivered of an ordinary pedigree Ayrshire calf and she never saw Ferdinand again. Mott managed to acquire a sturdy female bison and although she had to flirt outrageously to attract her mate's attention, eventually Ferdinand forgot about his first love and settled down to breed lots of little bison of his own.

By 1963 more than a million people a year were visiting Chester Zoo and while most of them came for pleasure, for a day's outing, there were more than a thousand parties of schoolchildren on educational trips. Keepers usually escort these trips and tell the children about the animals they see, answering their questions about biological and geographical backgrounds. For older pupils the zoo vet takes over, and many zoologists ask permission to spend weeks at a time in the zoo studying one particular animal about which they are preparing a thesis.

Essentially a practical man, Mott is frequently bewildered by misconceptions which are accepted as fact by some specialists. One such man arrived from Utrecht. He was writing a paper on the throwing ability of chimpanzees and wished to study those at Chester Zoo because they were particularly well-developed animals on account of the natural conditions on their island. While Mott was escorting the visitor on his first day, he listened in wonder to the conclusions that chimps always throw in the same manner, with an overarm movement.

At last he could keep silent no longer.

'That may be true of your chimps in Holland,' said Mott, 'but it certainly isn't true of these here. They each have different ways, and they frequently try new ones.'

The Dutchman smiled patiently, and as they came to a halt at the edge of the chimpanzee moat, he spoke at length and in great technical detail, peppered with Latin, of the bone structure that compelled chimpanzees always to throw overhand. From the corner of his eye, Mott saw Prince digging up a clump of earth, taking aim and letting fly—underarm. It sailed right between the two men, spattering their faces with mud. Not at all put out that his theory had just been demolished, the Dutchman assured Mott that it was just by accident that the chimp had managed to throw an underarm shot, that in actual fact, it was an impossibility.

Mott conceded that perhaps technical details could prove the impossibility, adding that according to the laws of aerodynamics, a bumblebee was so constructed that it could not possibly fly. Animals, he concluded, frequently make monkeys out of scientists.

But some visitors genuinely come to learn from the animals. When United States Government officials decided to set up a colony of chimpanzees in preparation for experiments in sending animals up into space, they made enquiries about zoos with the best records in rearing healthy animals. As a result they came to Chester to see for themselves Mott's revolutionary method of confining them on an island. They took aerial photographs showing the lay-out in relation to the rest of the zoo and made searching inspections into the chimps' health records, weight and height and tested the standard of their alertness and general intelligence. The results were so impressive that when they returned to America they set about building a replica of Chester's chimp island, but instead of its being half an acre, it was at least forty, and their chimps are not idlers and layabouts, but potential astronauts being trained to withstand the rigours of outer space and, perhaps, the moon.

If Chester's chimps do nothing else, they are a never-ending source of amusement to Mott. When foreign zoo officials visit him, he delights in strolling round the grounds with them and leading them, without warning, to the narrowest part of the moat where they come face to face with a family of chimps, only a few feet away. Time after time he has seen his visitors falter and gasp, then grab his arm and prepare to run for it, believing that the animals have escaped, and not noticing the moat that keeps them safely confined. That experienced zoo officials can be unaware, even momentarily, of barriers between animal and man, is the finest tribute that Mott can receive. Then he knows he has succeeded in what he set out to do.

CHAPTER FIFTEEN

A PRIDE OF LIONS

All members of the cat family have to be quarantined for six months when they arrive in Britain, and when Chester's cat population outgrew its accommodation, Mott decided to build a new type of house that could be so isolated from other buildings that it would be acceptable to the Ministry of Agriculture as a place where newcomers could be quarantined, instead of having to stay in Ministry accommodation many miles from the zoo.

The advantages were multiple; animals could be on view right from the time of their arrival, protected by armour-plated glass from all contact with both the public and other animals. Individual attention could be given to each animal and, in the event of the immigrants being pregnant on arrival, their young could be inoculated against that great killer of cats, feline distemper.

The house was two hundred feet long by fifty-five feet wide, divided down the middle by a ten-foot wide passageway flanked on either side by the animals' sleeping dens, all centrally heated. The outside enclosures were fronted with armour-plated glass and they were roofed with wire netting to prevent leaps to freedom. One side of the house was reserved for the larger animals such as leopards, jaguars and pumas, while the other was occupied by smaller species, caracal lynxes and jungle cats.

Few of the cat family will live peaceably with each other, most of them coming together at mating times and returning to a solitary existence afterwards. When cubs are born, the father must be removed in good time or he would attack and kill his young. But usually the mother cares for her cubs with fanatical devotion and would defend them to the death. An exception was a caracal lynx that dumped her kitten in the open enclosure and left it to die. The keeper rescued it and put it in a box with a blanket and a hot water bottle. He had to feed it on milk every four hours from a syringe fitted with a tiny rubber teat, and because it had to be fed regularly right round the clock, he took it home with him each night and put it in a box beside his bed, with an alarm clock to awaken him for the early morning feeds.

Some kittens become quite tame soon after birth and can be handled and weighed after their mothers are enticed into their open enclosures and locked away from the inner dens for a few minutes. The keepers must be very quick, however, and must not handle the cubs too much or the mother will find they have acquired a human smell and will have nothing more to do with them.

When Chester bred its first black panther cubs, a very rare event in any zoo, the cubs were vicious from the moment of birth. They had to be injected against feline enteritis at seven weeks and again at nine weeks and keepers had to help the vet hold the tiny spitting animals. Even at that tender age they had wicked claws and needle-sharp teeth plus an inborn hatred of man.

The house was built with twenty-six separate enclosures and had at one end a food preparation kitchen complete with its own deep-freeze, a cold storage room, and tables for cutting up food. Like domestic cats, the wild members took time to settle down in their new home. For days they paced backwards and forwards, hissing and spitting when visitors approached. But once they accepted the move, they rapidly developed a blind spot for the armour-plated glass through which the visitors look. No matter how people try to attract their attention by gesticulating or even tapping on the glass, the inmates seldom acknowledge their presence and frequently turn their backs to the public, proving how secure they must feel.

But lions have a different set of natural laws. They prefer to live in a pride of two or three males and half a dozen females. In the last thirty years, Chester Zoo has bred over seven hundred lions, and with so many examples to study Mott feels he understands them.

When the female goes into her den to have cubs, it's a brave male that dares to go near. The lioness has considerably more courage than her mate. It is she who does the hunting in the wild state, she who actually makes the kill, and never let the male forget it! The only male lion that ever proved the exception was Patrick, the male that came from Dublin when the zoo first started to found Chester's remarkable lion colony. He fathered nearly a hundred litters and when the cubs were only a day or two old he took over his share of baby-sitting with surprising gentleness and even more surprising acceptance by the females. Another lion that tried to emulate him was badly mauled by his mate and had to be locked in his den for weeks until his wounds healed. Once the mother brings her young into the open, the father is allowed to take an interest, and both parents usually share the training of the cubs. They begin by stalking father's tail as he swings it from side to side. Sometimes they pounce on it a little too vigorously and are rewarded by a swipe from his paw that sends them flying. And when the daily ration of horsemeat or chicken is thrown in, the cubs will play at fighting for it long before they are weaned.

Because lions in their natural state kill, eat and then rest before making another kill, Mott makes Fridays a 'no feeding' day for the lions. He chose Friday back in the 1930s because it was the day with the fewest visitors, and although this is no longer the case, the rule still holds. It is hard on those who come specially to see the lions fed, but it is responsible for the magnificent condition of the pride, most of which can expect a healthy life lasting twenty years or more.

Lionesses that were born in Chester Zoo and have known no other life never tire of watching the visitors. When the zoo appointed a security officer who patrolled the grounds night and day with an Alsatian dog on a leash, the lions used to wait for his approach when the whole pride would rush over to the wire and walk alongside man and dog until they had passed the enclosure. The dog was rather nervous at first and even when he became accustomed to the rush of lions, he never went nearer their paddock than he had to.

As well as a number of trees in their enclosure, there it a large log platform in the centre of the paddock where they can lie when the ground is damp. But most of them are so hardy that they enjoy rolling in the snow in the depth of winter and they seldom seek the shelter of their dens unless it is pouring with rain.

Their amiable appearance can prove disastrous if it is taken at face value. A keeper, believing his charges to be as friendly as they looked, carelessly entered one of the dens without first having made sure that the inmate was locked in the enclosure beyond. The full-grown lion was, in fact, resting in the shade of his den and as soon as the keeper walked in the lion was the more startled of the two. He sprang to his feet and pounced on the keeper, knocking him to the ground and raking his claws the length of the man's back. The lion then backed away, his claws dripping blood, and prepared to attack again. The moment's delay gave the keeper time to rush out of the den and lock the door behind him. He was badly injured and spent months in hospital; when he recovered he found that he had lost his nerve and could not face wild animals again.

Lions exercise a fascination for girl keepers who invariably ask if they can look after them. But only men are put in charge of the bigger animals that might possibly need manhandling in case of an escape or an attack. Even in men, Mott finds a reluctance to accept animals as wild creatures that have no wish to be tamed. In some cases the animal develops an affinity with its keeper but Mott does not like this to become too strong. The dangers of an animal becoming dependent on one man are obvious; the man might leave or be off sick, causing distress to the animal. Accordingly, keepers are regularly transferred to other departments so that they are familiar with several types of animals and so that strong personal attachments between man and beast cannot be formed.

But lions and polar bears, instead of growing fond of their keepers, invariably take a great dislike to them no matter how kind, patient and gentle they may be. They would gladly bite the hand that feeds them and they make no secret of their antipathy. When lions have to be enticed into their dens and locked in for a while so that workmen can do essential repairs and maintenance in the enclosure, it is almost impossible for the lion-keeper to coax them in. They will line up, snarling and spitting at him, ignoring the extra hunks of meat he offers them. Usually the lion-keeper enlists the aid of the polar bear-keeper who has exactly the same difficulty with his animals. And the lions come like lambs for the stranger, trotting obediently into their dens without a flick of the tail. Meanwhile the polar bears go through the same routine, accepting the lion-keeper and detesting their own. Both keepers agree that if one of their animals were to escape, it would ignore members of the public and make a bee-line for the keeper as victim number one.

Monkeys become very attached to individual keepers and some show a decided preference for girls. Early in the zoo's history many of the babies were abandoned by their mothers, perhaps because the conditions for breeding were not ideal. Bringing up infant monkeys is almost as onerous as rearing children, and even when it is done with devotion, hand-reared animals never quite catch up with those raised by their mothers. Both physically and mentally they lack the stamina which seems to be imbibed along with mothers' milk.

When there was sufficient money for Mott to build a new monkey house, he planned it to be as perfect in its way as the elephant house and the tropical house. Once again he separated the animals from the visitors by glass and the building was not only centrally heated, but air-conditioned. Fresh air was drawn in at one end of the house, filtered of its fog and dust, heated and then drawn out at the other end. The monkeys were installed according to the amount of warmth they required, the hardy ones being at the end where the warm air was withdrawn. The whole building was planted with tropical and semi-tropical plants with violent splashes of colour, and some species, including bougainvillaea, now flower twice a year.

Immediately the animals took up residence in the new house their health improved dramatically. There were no more epidemics of colds and chest troubles that kill so many captive monkeys, and the constant temperatures helped the babies to survive.

Monkeys and apes vary enormously in their capacity

to love or care for their offspring, and among baboons kidnapping by the over-maternal is all too common. When Trixie, a Barbary ape born in Chester Zoo, gave birth to Squeaker, she showed every sign of becoming an ideal mother. She fed and groomed her baby and held it out for the other apes to admire. One of them, Ginger, became envious and started following mother and child around, peering into the baby's face and tentatively touching its head. At first Trixie snatched her baby away and hid it in her arms, but after a few days she became less suspicious. Ginger seized the opportunity, grabbed Squeaker from her mother and raced to the far end of the cage holding the baby in one arm while fending off the outraged Trixie with the other. Attracted by the row, the keeper entered the cage to restore the baby to its rightful owner. Ginger flew at his face when he removed Squeaker and screamed in rage. Like a child in a tantrum, she beat her head against the wall while Trixie, her child restored to her, sat smugly on the perch, rocking gently backwards and forwards.

When Ginger seemed to have quietened down, the keeper opened the door to leave, and before he realised what was happening, Ginger had dashed through and escaped into the open. The last he saw of her was a flash of fur disappearing rapidly through the bushes. A general alarm was put out, but no one in the zoo had seen the little ape, and although the search went on all that day and the next, there was no sign of her anywhere. Two days later came a report of something furry sitting on a roof top half a mile away. It was Ginger. Keepers went along with a bag of fruit and titbits, but she refused to come down. She was obviously cold and very hungry, but even more determined not to be recaptured.

As a last resort, one of the keepers returned to the zoo and brought baby Squeaker out as bait. Ginger came down at once and was allowed to cuddle the baby all the way back to the monkey house, where it was given back to its mother while Ginger was put in a separate cage. On her own, she sulked and fretted, while Trixie had lost interest in her child and couldn't be bothered feeding it. If the infant had been weaned it would have been a simple matter of letting Ginger adopt it. But Squeaker was too young so neither ape was allowed to keep her, and she was transferred to a nursery cage where she could be bottle fed along with Mathilda, a baby olive baboon.

Mathilda had been a healthy baby at birth, but within a few days she had begun to fail. Mott advised the keeper to keep a close watch on mother and child to see how they were getting on. He hid behind a section of plants and waited to see how the baby was being cared for. As soon as she thought the keeper had gone, the mother looked round furtively to see if any visitors were about. When she saw no one, she began plucking tufts of hair out of the baby's head. She allowed it to suckle, but as soon as its mouth was full of milk, she clapped its cheeks to make it spit it out. After a few minutes of this, the baby was too exhausted and discouraged to suck any longer.

Mathilda was taken away from her mother. She was a very shy baboon and although she and Squeaker became the best of friends, she was incurably jealous. If visitors or keepers made more fuss of Squeaker than of her, she reacted by attacking her friend and banging on the glass to send the visitors away.

Motherhood helped a ring-tailed lemur to stop pining for the past. Tweet had been a house pet before she was presented to the zoo and she nearly died of grief during her first few weeks. She was in such a state of prostration that in the beginning the keeper took her home with him every night in order to soften the shock of being parted from her owner. For months she refused to look at other lemurs and in the end it was only loneliness that made her accept a place in their cage. Once her nightly trips ended she had made a wall of reserve around herself. She ignored all humans, resented them for their fickleness. At times she peered through her window, wistfully watching the happier cages where groups of monkeys played games among themselves.

When she was put in the cage with three other lemurs, she was afraid at first and kept well away from them. Gradually, however, she began to take an interest and soon became one of the family. A year later she nearly fell off the perch in surprise when she gave birth to a baby. In her excitement, she forgot her mistrust of the keeper and held out the tiny creature to show him. She became a different animal as she learnt how to care for the infant. From now on she had no need of humans and no hankering to return to the past. She was genuinely sorry when the baby stopped clinging to the soft fur of her stomach and began moving independently. She remained full of pride for it, and Mott let it stay with her even when it was grown up, as a symbol that some things, even in a zoo, could be permanent.

CHAPTER SIXTEEN

A HAPPY MAN

Now that Chester Zoo has an income approaching three-quarters of a million pounds a year and increasing annually, its future progress is assured. Enclosures are constantly being enlarged, buildings redesigned and rebuilt to incorporate methods which current research suggests might be better for the animals. There is a new apehouse with its own islands, a large free-flight aviary and a unique parrot house, vast paddocks for bison, antelopes and zebra and the building programme is endless. Mr Mottershead and his staff are always at work examining new and better ways of housing the animals.

Many of the keepers choose to spend their holidays visiting foreign zoos to study and compare conditions. In 1973 the Curator of Mammals and Birds, Mr Bill Timmis, was given leave of absence to visit the Indonesian islands of Bali, Flores and Komodo where he could gain first-hand knowledge of the requirements of tropical birds and reptiles in their natural habitat, knowledge that could help to make life in Chester Zoo more satisfactory for many creatures. Mr Mottershead has not had a holiday for the past forty-three years that has not incorporated visits to zoos, wildlife reserves or animals in their natural surroundings.

Unlike many zoos, Chester receives no grants from government bodies, local authorities or businesses, and relies entirely on the 45p a head entrance fee. And all the profits are ploughed back into the development of the zoo.

If it is an outstanding success drawing more than a million visitors a year, it is because people feel they are getting their money's worth. More and more schools from as far afield as Scotland, South Wales, the East coast and the Midlands bring parties of children not just for a pleasant day out in beautiful surroundings, but to see for themselves how animal communities live. In 1972 more than 3,000 such parties came, and the numbers rise annually.

In the quiet of the evening when most of the visitors have gone, Mott makes his way round the zoo seeing constant reminders of the half of his life he has lived there. The old lions' den, now a storehouse, was built in the early years when he had to do all the manual work himself, with only a chimpanzee to help. Mary was as good as any labourer, she could mix mortar, fetch and carry and even lay some of the bricks. She was good company, too, and did her bit towards making the zoo what it is today.

The two restaurants and three cafeterias are a far cry from the cafe run entirely by Mrs Mottershead and the two children. The evenings were never restful in those days, for when the last visitor had gone, Mrs Mottershead had to handwash all the tablecloths and tea towels in readiness for the next day. The cages had to be cleaned out—they couldn't be done during visiting hours—and it was seldom possible for Mr and Mrs Mottershead to finish their work before midnight.

Now there is a staff of 400 men and women but Mott still works a seven-day week and knows every one of the 841 mammals, the 1,644 birds and 184 reptiles. He confesses that he cannot recognise all the thousands of fish.

The original nine acres have become 335, the animals' annual food bill which came to £250 in 1932, now exceeds £45,000, and the value of the zoo, lock, stock and barrel runs into many millions of pounds. The pair of Mountain Gorillas, bought for £3,500, are now worth over £25,000, a sum Mr Motterhead recently turned down. To him they are beyond price, and certainly not for sale.

So valued are the animals bred in Chester, for their health and stamina, that they are in demand all over the world. They have been exchanged for other species or sold to zoos on every continent. A rhinoceros went to Moscow, lions to South Africa, zebras to New Zealand, leopards to Canada, coaties to Rangoon, birds to East Berlin, Père David's deer to West Germany, a llama to France . . . the list is endless.

In some species the breeding has become so prolific that it becomes almost an embarassment. The colony of ten marmots—or prairie dogs—acquired in 1965, grew to over a hundred four years later. Probably no zoo in Britain (or Europe) has bred and reared so many chimpanzees, and the Talapoin monkey which seldom breeds in other zoos, produces healthy young at frequent intervals.

Bears, wallabies, penguins, giraffes, lions and tigers increase almost every year in Chester Zoo and it has an impressive record of 'first time' births in captivity in British and even world zoos. Impressive, too, is its record in animal parents rearing their young, for although captive creatures will sometimes breed, they often refuse to rear the infants unless conditions are exactly what they need to make them happy and secure.

Many of the animal characters of the early years have gone. Barbar, survivor of the anthrax epidemic, died of old age last year. She was well over 40, and as she lay dying, the young bull Nobby which had come to the zoo as a lonely two-year-old and had been mothered by her, tried to blow air into her mouth with his trunk. He was desolate for days.

Ferdinand, the wandering bison, left behind him a sturdy family of children and grandchildren, some of them scattered all over the world. Of the original five chimps, Simon, Solomon, Elmer, Meg and Babu which helped to pioneer the system of island enclosures, only Meg is left. A little grey around the muzzle and not quite so sprightly, she still produces a baby nearly every year—she became a grandmother last year (1973) and she still manages a hand-stand when Mott passes by; and showers him with sods of earth.

The 1960s and '70s saw great advances. The first Bird of Paradise—the Superb—hatched and reared a chick. Numerous other rare species were bred.

A laboratory was built where preventive medicine could be practised and where specimens from sick animals could be examined rapidly lest any infection was present and the patient had to be isolated. Doctors and scientists from Liverpool and Manchester Universities co-operate, to the mutual advantage of all parties.

International film and television companies include Chester in their round of the world's best zoos and a constant stream of eminent zoologists endorse the opinion. Students gain doctorates after studying groups of animals living as though they were in the wild—but far more accessible. At least one foreign king has gone through the turnstiles, and in April 1972 the Duke of Edinburgh made his first formal visit to open the 174-seat lecture hall and library where members of the Society can hear talks by leading experts and read specialised books which are selected to further the knowledge of animal behaviour and their welfare.

When sculptor Sean Rice won the Constance prize for his 'Noah', he chose Chester Zoo as the most appropriate site for its permanent home in preference to one of the London Parks. When the sixteen-foot sculpture has been cast in bronze, probably in 1975, it will be placed in the new sunken garden which used to be called the Donkeys' Nest.

On the face of it much has changed, yet fundamentally Chester Zoo is the same as it always was. Mr Mottershead's original aims, formulated so long ago, still obtain. The zoo is dedicated to the preservation of wildlife, to maintaining the dignity and fulfilment of all creatures and to educating the public to a deeper understanding of nature. Always the balance is kept to put the animals' welfare first but at the same time permitting the visitors to observe them without the hindrance of bars or intrusive fences. More and more paddocks are being surrounded by sunken ditches bordered by low stone walls, like a dry moat. The animals find shelter in the hollows in windy weather and the public have excellent visibility without obstructions.

Although in his late seventies, Mr Mottershead still goes round the zoo every day—sometimes by car—and keeps track of the health of every animal. A sea-lion's bark will take him back through the years to the time when local residents complained that it was disturbing their sleep. It is sometimes an effort to come back to the present as he looks down at the children who often accompany him, not his daughters, Muriel and June, but his grandchildren, Joy, Linda and five-year old George.

The window of his flat in Oakfield looks out on to the beautiful rock garden in which is placed a plaque:

ERECTED BY THE COUNCIL OF THE NORTH OF ENGLAND ZOOLOGICAL SOCIETY IN MEMORY OF ELIZABETH MOTTERSHEAD, 1887–1969, WIFE OF THE FOUNDER OF CHESTER ZOO, AS A TOKEN OF GRATITUDE FOR HER

FORTY YEARS OF CONTINUOUS EFFORT AND DEVOTION IN
ESTABLISHING THE ZOOLOGICAL GARDENS.

For so many years of work and worry, his rewards, materially, have been less than lavish. An honorary degree of Master of Science was conferred on him in 1964 by Manchester University; the OBE which the Queen awarded him in the 1973 New Year's Honours, a modest flat inside the zoo and the title of Director-Secretary which he has had since the Society was formed. But George Saul Mottershead will die a happy man. Not only has he provided pleasure and enlightenment for millions of people, but in so doing, he has immeasurably improved the lot of captive animals in zoos all over the world. Where he led, others followed, to the advantage of caged creatures everywhere.

LOOKING AND FINDING
by Geoffrey Grigson 25p

552 54007 2 Carousel Non-Fiction

You can find sunken treasure, hidden away in some long-forgotten shipwreck, or discover the past through scattered fossils and ancient inscriptions. It depends what you're looking for, how you go about finding it. It depends where you're looking, how you go about getting there. But once the search begins, there's no knowing what you might stumble across.

THE WHITE BADGER
by Gordon Burness 25p

552 54008 0 Carousel Non-Fiction

A badger was born just outside London, in fact only eighteen miles from the city centre. He was discovered by eleven year old Gary and his older brother Phil, who had arrived one day at the author's doorstep with a request to be taken badger hunting. Their first find was unusual, for it wasn't an ordinary badger, it was all-white, an albino badger. Gary called him Snowball, and this is his story.

NATURE DETECTION AND CONSERVATION
by Jean Mellanby 25p

552 54019 6 Carousel Non-Fiction

Nature and wild life are today threatened by a variety of man-made dangers such as industrial pollution. This serious problem has baffled our top scientists and politicians. Yet there is plenty that you can do about it, and this book shows how we can all become nature detectives and help preserve wild life, even if we live in the heart of a city. And we can enjoy doing so.

JASON
by Joyce Stranger 20p

552 52004 7 Carousel Fiction

The pup wasn't wanted, born of a golden Labrador bitch and a giant mastiff. Then Duncan found him, a lonely young boy who needed a friend just as much as Jason needed a loving owner. The closeness between them was only strengthened when Duncan was sent away to school, and then his father had an accident; Jason had to do something.

THE MODEL-RAILWAY MEN
by Ray Pope 25p

552 52024 1 Carousel Fiction

Mark operates his model railway as near to the real thing as possible. Then he encounters the Telford family, miniature people who live only for the railway—Mark's railway. The adventures of Mark and his live passengers will be enjoyed by anyone who has known the delights of a model railway.

HOW AND WHY WONDER BOOK OF THE HUMAN BODY 25p

552 86504 4 Carousel Non-Fiction

Knowledge of the human body's structure and functioning is essential for healthy living. Moreover, it is a fascinating field of study. Here is an informed and easy to read account of the body's working, reproduction, and how to maintain personal well-being. Illustrations enhance the text.

All these books are available at your bookshop or can be ordered direct from Transworld Publishers Ltd., Cash Sales Dept., P.O. Box 11, Falmouth, Cornwall.

Please send full name and address together with cheque or postal order—no currency, and allow 7p per book to cover the cost of postage and packing.

If you would like to receive a newsletter telling you about our new children's books, send your name and address to Gillian Osband, Transworld Publishers Ltd., 57/59 Uxbridge Road, Ealing, London, W5, and mention 'CHILDREN'S NEWSLETTER'.